THE GREAT CANADIAN
LITERARY
COOKBOOK

THE GREAT CANADIAN
LITERARY
COOKBOOK

Introduction by Peter Gzowski

Illustrations by Kim LaFave

Published by

The Festival Of The Written Arts,

SECHELT, BRITISH COLUMBIA

Canadian Cataloguing in Publication Data
The Great Canadian literary cookbook

Includes index.
ISBN 0-9698173-1-2

1. Cookery, Canadian. I. Southin, Gwendolyn. II. Keller, Betty. III. Festival of the Written Arts (Sechelt, B.C.)
TX715.6.G73 1994   641.5971   C94-910259-8

Designed by Roger Handling, Glassford Design

Illustrations by Kim la Fave

Cover Design by Roger Handling and Kim la Fave

The Sunshine Coast Festival of the Written Arts
Box 2299,
Sechelt, B.C. V0N 3A0
Phone 604-885-9631 Fax: 604-885-3967

Printed in Canada by Friesen Printers Ltd.

TABLE OF CONTENTS

FOREWORD

The idea of a Festival of the Written Arts Cookbook was born on a hot August evening in 1986 when Gwen Southin and Betty Keller found themselves—the last of the Festival clean-up crew—mopping floors after all the events were over for another year. Everyone else had gone home, sated with great literature and good food. Mops in hand, our char ladies pondered the weekend's events.

"One day," Betty said, "we should write a book about this."

"One day," Gwen replied, "we should write a cookbook with all the recipes we serve here!"

By the time they finished mopping the floors, it had been decided: one day they would write a cookbook and include recipes from all the Festival's speakers and some of the recipes served at the Festival and at our writing workshops, and this marvellous cookbook would be featured at the Festival.

The years went by. We moved the Festival to the Rockwood Centre, built our beautiful Pavilion, and each year we featured another prominent cookbook author. But 1994 is the year of the Festival cookbook! We've gathered recipes from 65 of our past speakers and we present them here along with a selection of our own Festival specialties.

This book would not have been possible without the labour of the Cookbook Project Committee: Marla Chatham, Kay Bellinger, Peggy Treloar, Gail Bull, Maureen Foss, Rosella Leslie, and Eileen Williston, and the guidance of the Festival's publishing specialist, Earl Schmidt.

And our special appreciation goes out to all the authors who accepted our kitchen stove challenge. Thank you. We hope you enjoy *The Great Canadian Literary Cookbook*.

The Editors
Gwendolyn Southin & Betty Keller
February 5, 1994

PETER GZOWSKI

Peter Gzowski, friend to all of Canada's writers, also knows a great deal about cooking and good food—he is, by his own admission, the world's greatest gazpacho maker—and that is one reason why, when he so kindly offered to contribute an introduction to **The Great Canadian Literary Cookbook**, we accepted with alacrity. The other reason is that Peter, twice a guest speaker at the Festival of the Written Arts, is regarded around here as somewhat of a patron saint.

This summer of 1994 he completes his twelfth year as host of CBC Radio's *Morningside*, the program that *Maclean's* magazine called "the best and most Canadian thing in Canadian broadcasting, radio or television". For three hours every weekday morning, *Morningside* is broadcast from coast-to-coast in a feast of intelligent, engaging conversations, debates, personal essays, music and drama. "The listeners are my guides to what I'm doing right or wrong," says Peter Gzowski, who starts his day by reading his listeners' mail responses. "The audience is part of the program in many ways."

Peter Gzowski began his writing career at 19 at the Timmins *Daily Press* between the two halves of his education at the University of Toronto, where he became editor of *The Varsity*. After university, he became the city editor of the Moose Jaw *Times-Herald*, then managing editor of the Chatham *Daily News*. In 1956 he joined the staff at *Maclean's* magazine, becoming at age 28 its youngest managing editor.

Peter's radio career was launched in 1969; two years later he became host of *This Country in the Morning*. From 1976 to 1978 he hosted CBC-TV's *90 Minutes Live*. He took a break from broadcasting in 1978 to devote the next four years to writing, producing several best-selling books, a daily column for the Toronto Star, and award-winning articles.

Since returning to radio to host *Morningside* in 1982, he has published six more books, including the bestselling, **Fourth Morningside Papers** (1992) and **Canadian Living: Selected Columns** (McClelland & Stewart, 1993). For two seasons he was also host of CBC-TV's *Gzowski & Co.*, a series of programs on Canadian achievers.

In 1986 he began hosting the Peter Gzowski Invitational Golf Tournaments for Literacy. The tournaments are now held annually on fourteen sites from Fredericton to Baffin Island to Saskatoon and Victoria with stops in between, but they are golf tournaments with a difference because as well as golf, they feature poetry and fiction readings and live music. As of October 1993, he became honourary chairman of the tournaments in order to give himself more time for writing.

Peter Gzowski has won seven ACTRA awards, received honorary degrees from seven Canadian universities and in 1986 was named a member of the Order of Canada.

Festival 3 (1985) & 10 (1992)

INTRODUCTION

BY PETER GZOWSKI

My favourite way of getting to the Sechelt Festival of the Written Arts is to show up at a dock I know in Vancouver harbour, and hop a sea-plane flown by a guy named Klaus. Klaus flies you the scenic route. Every flight path between Vancouver and the Sechelt peninsula is stunning, of course: mountains and islands and the sun glimmering off the waters of Howe Sound. But Klaus's own joy in the trip he has made a thousand times adds to his passengers' pleasure, and by the time his magic carpet, after a few swoops down to check out the hovercraft on its way to Victoria, or to see if Bruno Gerussi's out sunbathing at his house at Gibson's Landing, settles into your destination, you feel as if you can't help but have a good time.

The pleasure rolls on when you're ashore. Writers come from all over the country to gather at Sechelt. You never know who you'll run into. You never know what they'll do either. Ostensibly, we're all there to read and be read to. But when someone like Tom Berger, say, steps to the podium in the airy and spacious outdoor pavilion, set among the cedars and the firs, his talk is liable to turn into a stimulating hour-long seminar on the future of Canada, with people hanging on every word (I eavesdropped on that session from the balcony of my room in the Rockwood Centre). Or when Lorna Crozier opens her latest book of poems (Lorna actually followed Tom one year, as I remember), it can take off into a session from which the laughter wafts out over the salty air, and people call out requests like patrons in a familiar bar.

Before and after—and, if the truth be known, sometimes during—the formal sessions, there's still more talk. Breakfast, lunch and supper (all one form or another of buffet) are constant colloquies. So are the breaks. If none of the conversations at any of the umbrellaed tables strikes your fancy, you just take your tea somewhere else amid the rhodendrons and magnolias and settle down. Soon, someone will join you. Everyone—writers, patrons, volunteers (when they have time) and just passers-by—feels free to drop in on everyone else. I remember once, right after I'd dropped out of the sky in Klaus's plane, checking into my room and, just to make sure I could do some entertaining during my stay, heading out for the local emporium to pick up a bottle of wine. On my way I met the poet Patrick Lane. We shopped together and decided to hit the beach. There, as we parked on a log and watched the breakers roll in while we solved the problems of the world, Jeffrey Simpson, *The Globe and Mail's* keenest political writer, came strolling down the path. We waved him over, and for much of the next three hours, the poet, the pundit and the broadcaster talked of baseball, boyhood, landscape, friendship and—well, okay—women. I can't think of anywhere else in the world where three such disparate people could have done that.

THIS LOVELY BOOK is as varied and unpredictable as a visit to Sechelt itself, with recipes that range from the sublime (see Umberto Menghi's osso buco, for example, or try to read about Robert Kroetsch's tyropitta without your mouth watering) to the. . . well, to Robin Skelton's. It has therapeutic soups, tangy salads and desserts that should probably be illegal. It has childhood memories, family secrets, kitchen misadventures and a fish ceviche (from Paul St. Pierre) that sounds as if it would cure pneumonia.

The only thing I can think of, in fact, that could be more seductive than spending some time contemplating its charms—and sampling them—would be heading down to that dock again, and seeing if Klaus is idling his engine.

PART ONE
OUR WRITERS' RECIPES

TRYSH ASHBY-ROLLS

For most of her life, former broadcast journalist Trysh Ashby-Rolls hid the secrets of her childhood from friends, family and even herself. But spinal cord surgery triggered memories of being sexually abused by her father, who had even used her in a child pornography ring when she was eleven years old. **Triumph: A Journey of Healing from Incest** (McGraw-Hill Ryerson, 1991) is the step-by step account of her growth from victim to survivor as she rescued herself from the nightmare that had been her childhood. She has appeared on national and regional television and in person to speak about healing from childhood sexual abuse and incest.

In the early 1980s Trysh Ashby-Rolls took "one of those do-it-yourself-overnight courses" in broadcast journalism taught by executive producers from the CBC. From it she learned how to rewrite wire service copy and began visiting tv stations where she watched, asked questions and learned.

Five months later she became Canada's first paid news director and anchor in the cable television industry. She moved on to CHCH-TV and the CBC to produce current affairs programs. In 1982 she won an Award of Merit for Responsible and Supportive Journalism from Toronto's Emily Stowe Shelter for Women.

She moved to B.C.'s Sunshine Coast in 1989. Her training and practice in the field of prenatal education and counselling brought her a Certificate of Achievement in Child Sexual Abuse Intervention in 1991. She now facilitates support and education groups for adult female survivors and has trained mental health professionals from coast to coast on how to work with survivors. Her next book, **Take Care of Yourself While You Heal: A Practical Guide for Survivors**, will appear in 1994.
Festival 10 (1992)

Sandwiched between a career as an educator and counsellor in the seventies and a journalistic career in the following decade, I ran my own specialty baking business. Every weekday morning for two years, I baked a gross or two of muffins and dozens of loaves of bread in the back of a small bakery in the east end of Toronto. Then I headed downtown to deliver them to several gourmet food stores, including Holt Renfrew. I can claim full responsibility for being the first to put zucchini muffins on the scene, and my herb and onion bread was such a hot item I once baked four hundred loaves for one order. It was much easier—and half as much fun— writing about food, which I did later for *à la carte* magazine.

ZUCCHINI MUFFINS

Pre-heat oven to 400° F. Prepare muffin pan. Yields one dozen muffins.

2 cups grated **zucchini** 500 ml	1 tsp **cinnamon** 5 ml
2 cups **wholewheat flour** 500 ml	1 cup **walnut pieces** 250 ml
2 cups **unbleached white flour** 500 ml	1 cup **raisins** 250 ml
2 tsp **baking powder** 10 ml	1 cup **oil** 250 ml
2 tsp **baking soda** 10 ml	3/4 cup melted **honey** 175 ml
1 tsp **salt** 5 ml	3 **large eggs**

- Peel the zucchini before grating it if it tastes bitter.
- Mix together first nine ingredients.
- In a separate bowl beat together the oil, eggs and honey.
- Pour into the dry ingredients. Stir quickly.
- Scoop into muffin cups.
- Bake 20 - 25 minutes.
- Cool on wire rack.

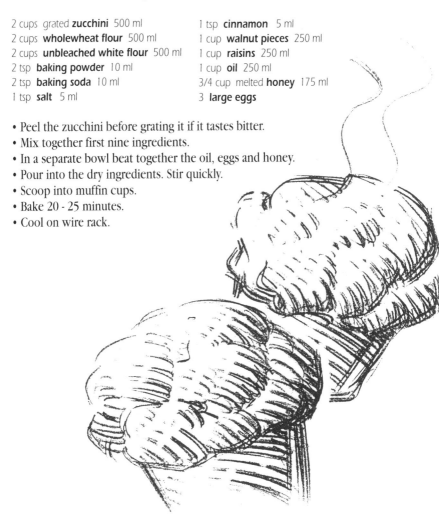

HERB 'N ONION BREAD

Preheat oven to 350°F. Grease a 9 x 5 x 3inch (23 x 12 x 7cm) loaf pan. Sprinkle cornmeal on the base (optional). Yields one small loaf.

1 package **quick acting dry yeast**
1 cup **warm water** 250 ml
1 tbsp **oil** 15 ml
1 tbsp melted **honey** 15 ml
1 cup **wholewheat flour** 250 ml
1 tsp **salt** 5 ml
1/2 tsp **rosemary** 2 ml
1 1/4 cups **unbleached white flour** 325 ml

1/2 tsp **basil** 2 ml
1/2 tsp **oregano** 2 ml
1/2 tsp **dill** 2 ml
1/4 tsp **sage** 1 ml
1/4 tsp **thyme** 1 ml
1 small **onion**, finely chopped
sesame or poppy seeds (optional)

• Dissolve yeast in warm water.
• Add melted honey and oil.
• Add flour, salt, onion and herbs.
• Beat mixture until smooth.
• Cover with a towel and put in warm place to rise about one hour.
• Punch batter down.
• Place in bread pan. Scatter with sesame or poppy seeds (optional).
• Let sit 10 minutes.
• Bake 50 minutes.
• Cool on a wire rack.

THOMAS R. BERGER

Thomas R. Berger, who practiced law in B.C. from 1956 to 1970, served in government for the NDP as a Member of Parliament and later as M.L.A., both times in Vancouver-Burrard. In 1971 he was appointed to the B.C. Supreme Court and during his time on the bench headed three royal commissions of inquiry.

The first was a commission on Family and Children's Law for the government of British Columbia which he carried out during 1973-4. For the next three years he led the Mackenzie Valley Pipeline Inquiry; his report, **Northern Frontier, Northern Homeland**, sold more copies than any other publication of the Canadian government. In 1979 he headed his third royal commission, this time on Indian and Inuit health care programs. His public intervention in 1981 (which was personally opposed by Prime Minister Trudeau) was nevertheless instrumental in the inclusion of aboriginal rights in the new Canadian Constitution. That same year he wrote **Fragile Freedoms**, a study of human rights and dissent in Canada.

Thomas Berger was chosen to head the Alaska Native Review Commission in 1983 and his report was published two years later as **Village Journey** (Hill and Wang). His most recent book, **A Long and Terrible Shadow** (Douglas and McIntyre, 1992) is an examination of European values and native rights in North and South America from 1492 to 1992. Since 1991 he has been Deputy Chairman of the first independent review commissioned by the World Bank to examine the implementation of resettlement and environmental measures in the multi-billion dollar Sardar Sarovar dam and irrigation projects in India. The 360-page report he authored with his U.S. colleague Bradford Morse was strongly critical of the World Bank's support of the project in part because it would displace nearly 100,000 people.

Thomas Berger received the Order of Canada in 1990. He now practices law in Vancouver.

Festival 10 (1992)

TOM'S TUCKER

1 paella pan (2-3 qts) or a metal pan with 3" sides.
1/4 cup **butter**
3 **eggs**
3/4 cup **milk**
3/4 cup **flour**
1 cup **mixed blueberries and raspberries, fresh or frozen.**

* Drain juice from fruit.
* Put butter in paella pan and place in pre-heated oven at 425° F.
* In food processor or electric mixer, beat eggs one at a time.
* Add milk.
* Gradually add flour, mixing all for 30 seconds.
* Pour batter over melted butter.
* Drop fruit over batter.
* Bake 15 - 25 minutes.

Other toppings could be peeled and sliced apples sprinkled with sugar and cinnamon.

A savoury option could be shredded cheese and 1 cup mixed sliced vegetables. Sprinkle with coarse ground pepper.

PIERRE *B* ERTON

Pierre Berton was born in 1920 and raised in the Yukon, working in Klondike mining camps during his university years. He spent 4 years in the army rising to captain/instructor at the Royal Military College in Kingston. He spent his early newspaper career in Vancouver where at 21 he became the youngest city editor on any Canadian daily. He moved to Toronto in 1947 and by age 31 had graduated to the job of managing editor of *Maclean's*. He joined the Toronto *Star* as associate editor and columnist in 1958, leaving four years later to commence his own television program *The Pierre Berton Show* which ran until 1973.

Now one of the most easily recognized literary personalities in Canada for his weekly appearances on CBC television's *Front Page Challenge* (after 37 years the longest running entertainment show in the country), Pierre Berton is renowned as the man who almost single-handedly convinced Canadians they really had a history. The author of more than 40 books, 3 of them winners of Governor General's Awards for creative non-fiction, Pierre Berton holds 2 National Newspaper Awards, 2 ACTRA "Nellies" for broadcasting, and 12 honorary degrees. He is a Companion of the Order of Canada and a member of the Canadian News Hall of Fame.

His most memorable books include **The Golden Trail** (1955), **The Mysterious North** (1956), **Klondike** (1958), **Just Add Water and Stir** (1959), **Adventures of a Columnist** (1960), **The Big Sell** (1963), **The Comfortable Pew** (1965), **The Centennial Food Guide** (1966), **The Smug Minority** (1968), **The National Dream** (1970), **The Last Spike** (1971), **Drifting Home** (1973), **The Dionne Years** (1977), **The Wild Frontier** (1978), **The Invasion of Canada** (1980), **The Klondike Quest** (1983), **The Promised Land** (1984), **Vimy** (1986), **Starting Out** (1987), **The Arctic Grail** (1988), **Niagara: A History of the Falls** (1992), and **A Picture Book of Niagara Falls** (1993).

His books for young people include his favourite book, **The Secret World of Og**, and his 20-volume Canadian History Series including: **Canada Under Seige**, **A Prairie Nightmare** and **The Capture of Detroit**. Festival 7(1989) & 10(1992)

CLAM CHOWDER (From his book **Just Add Water And Stir**)

Lunching in the Connaught-Sheraton Hotel in Hamilton one day, my eye was caught by the words "New England clam chowder" on the menu. As this magnificent dish is a rarity in restaurants, I ordered it instantly, my jaws slavering like those of a half-starved boarhound.

The waitress arrived presently with a bowl containing a pink and noxious fluid which I identified at once as Manhattan clam chowder, sometimes known as Coney Island clam chowder, an inferior compilation rendered hideous by the addition of tomatoes.

A giddiness came over me at this imposture and, insensate with rage, I seized an olive spear and sped toward the kitchen to confront the chef.

"Did you make clam chowder with tomatoes and advertise it as New England clam chowder?" I asked him.

"I did," the forger said, and without a second thought I stabbed him through his black heart. There was no blood in him; only tomato juice.

I surrendered to the gendarmerie at once and was dragged, unrepentant, before the magistrate.

"Why did you do it?" the kindly jurist asked.

"Because he made clam chowder with tomatoes," I answered in a ringing voice. Naturally, they set me free.

I have since been washing my mouth out with real New England clam chowder, sometimes known as Boston clam chowder, trying to rid my palate of the taint of the counterfeit brew. I have wallowed in about a gallon of it, hot with the fragrance of the sea, alive with juicy clams and chopped onions and tiny bits of bacon which gleam like small jewels in the thick succulence of the simmering tureen.

Oh sweet New England! Happy state to be so immortalized by association with this emperor among chowders! Even George the Third would forgive your treachery were he to sample this healing distillation of your ocean!

And if there are those in the audience who wish to follow me in a carnival of creation, let me put no obstacle in their way.

First, open two tins of butter clams. I know that real clams should be used, but this, alas, is Canada, and we do not get real clams in most of Canada. If you live on either coast, by all means use real clams. Otherwise,

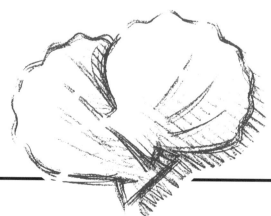

we must be content with the tinned variety.

Pour the clam nectar—but not the clams—into a saucepan and heat it up, adding at the same time about a cupful of clear chicken broth, a teaspoon of thyme, a teaspoon of celery salt, a teaspoon of paprika, and a teaspoon of ground fresh pepper. Dice two large potatoes and let them simmer in this pleasantly aromatic brew.

Chop two or three medium-sized onions and four or five slices of bacon. Now take the drained clams and separate the necks, which are the tough parts, from the clams proper. Chop up the necks with the bacon and onions and sautee them very gently with butter in a skillet. On no account let them brown or crisp.

As you do all this you will become aware of a subtle change in your kitchen. You are no longer in staid old Toronto, Saskatoon, Wetaskawin or Chilliwack, home of well-done roast beef and parsley potatoes. You are down where the relentless surf pounds like a lover's beating heart on the barnacled rocks, and the tall ships lean into the wind, and men in sou'westers trudge down to the seas again.

The chopped clams bubbling slightly among the onions and bacon and butter send up a bouquet which, mingling with the steam rising from the simmering and herbaceous nectar, brings memories of glistening beaches baking in the sun, far-off shores haunted by the ghosts of buccaneers, and stories by Stevenson and Captain Marryat. I cannot make clam chowder without recalling that scene of the Swiss Family Robinson's first night on their desert island, dipping shells into the hot brew that had been harvested from the garden of the sea.

When the onions are soft, dump the contents of the skillet into the saucepan with the clam nectar. Now add half a cup of dry white wine and let the whole mixture simmer very gently until the diced potatoes, too, are soft. Do not on any account let the chowder boil at a gallop; everything must be done reverently and with patience so that the nectar and the flavours mingle together. In making clam chowder, speed is a cardinal sin and we need to exercise that forbearance which was a quality of those Pilgrim Fathers who, I am certain, had their characters tempered by regular infusions of the New England brew.

When the potatoes are soft, add the whole clams and stir in two or three cups of milk, depending how thick you like your chowder. (If guests should suddenly drop in in large droves—a problem often encountered by chowder makers—just simply add more milk and more clams; chowder, after all, is an easily expandable dish.) You can use cream or whole milk, but I find partly skimmed evaporated milk (such as Farmer's Wife) just as good and perhaps better. Stir it in gently, too, so it doesn't curdle.

Now add a couple of pinches of Cayenne pepper and about a teaspoon of Madras curry powder. I have never seen this listed in a chowder recipe, but I can vouch for its effect. It seems to pull the chowder together and to enhance the clam flavour. Curry can be used for other things besides curries, if it is used sparingly, and chowder is one of them.

Now we have reached the most difficult part of all. To have really good chowder you should put it away and let it stand. Put it in the refrigerator and keep it cold, because of the milk it contains. Like mulligan and baked beans and many other dishes, it improves with age.

When you can stand it no longer, haul it out and get it piping hot. Crumble about a dozen salted soda crackers into the brew and let them soak well in. Then serve it up in big, deep bowls. This chowder is a meal by itself. All it needs to go with it is a glass of chilled white wine—a Sauterne, or a Chablis, or a Riesling. If you belong to the Women's Christian Temperance Union add a little soda water to the wine. That will make it temperate. You can do nothing with the Chowder itself, I fear. It is a most intemperate dish; after all, it was the food of pirates and freebooters and rebellious colonists of New England. Consume it at your peril.

A list of ingredients for your shopping guide:

2 tins **butter clams**	1 tsp **paprika**
1 cup **clear chicken broth**	1 tsp **ground fresh pepper**
3 med **onions**	1 tsp **Madras curry powder**
5 slices **bacon**	12 **salted soda crackers**
2 large **potatoes**	1/2 cup **dry white wine**
butter	2 - 3 cups **milk**
1 tsp **thyme**	**cayenne pepper**
1 tsp **celery salt**	

SANDRA BIRDSELL

Manitoba-born Sandra Birdsell, the child of a Metis Catholic father and a Mennonite mother, didn't begin writing until she was in her mid-thirties, prompted by the death of her father and the dawning realization of her own mortality. She began her training in a creative writing class at the University of Winnipeg with instructor James Walker who told the class that he believed there were probably only two real writers in the room. Birdsell's response was to wonder who the other one was. Later she studied with Robert Kroetsch at the University of Manitoba.

"Birdsell Revives Joy of Discovering Major New Talent," announced the headline over William French's 1982 *Globe and Mail* review when Sandra Birdsell's first collection of short stories, **Night Travellers**, (Turnstone) was published. When it was followed in 1984 by **Ladies Of The House** (Turnstone, 1984) Alberto Manguel told his *Books in Canada* readers that "these stories confirm Birdsell's position as one of the best short story writers in the language." Two years later the Canadian Book information Centre confirmed this by nominating her one of the country's 10 most promising writers by including her in their "45 Below" list. And when **The Agassiz Stories** (Turnstone), which combines both of the earlier books, was published in 1987, William French declared "Miss Birdsell has us well and truly hooked."

Her first novel, **The Missing Child**, which won the 1989 W.H. Smith/Books in Canada First Novel Award, was written while she did a two-year stint as Writer in Residence at the University of Waterloo. Her second novel, **The Chrome Suite**, finalist for the 1992 Governor General's Award for Fiction and the winner of the 1993 McNally Robinson Book of the Year Award, is a striking and original evocation of childhood. It was described by Geraldine Sherman in the *Globe and Mail* as "about as good as we're ever going to get."

She was given the Gerald Lampert Award for new fiction by the League of Canadian Poets and the National Magazine Award for short fiction, both in 1984. And in 1993 she received the Marian Engel Award in recognition of her significant contribution to Canadian literature. Her latest short stories were included in the 1993 Turnstone Press collection **Hearts Wild**.

Sandra Birdsell is also a successful playwright and scriptwriter; her scripts include a number for the critically acclaimed National Film Board Series, **Daughters of the Country** and two plays produced by the Prairie Theatre Exchange of Winnipeg.

Festival 8 (1990)

During the summer, every single Saturday we asked our mother, "So, what's for supper, eh?" And every single Saturday she would reply with a bit of annoyance, "We're having Summer Borscht and Zwieback." And of course, we screwed up our noses and said in one voice, "Ahhhh! Heck! Not soup and buns again!!"

Well, I realize now that the 'ahhh heck' soup and buns were very special indeed. The combination of Summer Borscht and Zwieback has regenerative qualities, the power to evoke strong memories and quite possibly great works of fiction. It most definitely creates the desire to climb up on your mother's lap.

MY MOTHER'S SUMMER BORSCHT

2 qts **soup stock made by boiling ham bone for 1 hour**
2 cups finely chopped **beet greens, burdock or sorrel leaves**
1/2 cup chopped **onion greens**
1/3 cup **dill greens**
3-4 medium **potatoes,** diced
salt and pepper to taste
1/2 cup **sweet cream**
1 cup **thick sour milk** (optional)

• Mix together soup stock and vegetables. Boil until vegetables are done.
• Add the cream and sour milk (optional) and serve hot.

ZWIEBACK

2 1/2 cups scalded **milk**
2 tsp **salt**
4 tbsp **sugar**
1 cup **shortening**

1/2 cup **warm water**
2 tsp **sugar**
1 cake **yeast**
2 **eggs** (optional)
8-10 cups **sifted flour**

• Scald milk, add shortening, salt and 4 tbsp sugar. Set aside until luke warm.
• Crumble yeast in small bowl, add 2 tsp sugar and 1/2 cup lukewarm water. Set in warm place until spongy.
• Add yeast mixture, and beaten eggs to lukewarm milk mixture.
• Mix well and stir in flour gradually.
• Knead dough until very soft and smooth.
• Cover and let rise in a warm place until double in bulk.
• Pinch off balls of dough the size of a small egg.
• Place balls 1 inch apart on greased pan.
• Put a similar ball, but slightly smaller, on top of bottom ball.
• Press down with thumb.
• Let rise until double in bulk (about 1 hour).
• Bake at 400°F to 425°F for 15 - 20 minutes.
Yields approximately 4 dozen.

GAIL BOWEN

Born in Toronto, a student of the Universities of Toronto, Waterloo and Saskatchewan, Gail Bowen moved to Saskatchewan for good in the late 1960s when her husband Ted became former Saskatchewan premier Allan Blakeney's speechwriter. She became an assistant professor of English at the Saskatchewan Indian Federated College (University of Regina), and at first limited her writing to scholarly articles and reviews.

But after she wrote the Saskatchewan entries for **An Easterner's Guide to Western Canada/A Westerner's Guide to Eastern Canada**, she decided to launch a literary career. Her first attempt was a novella co-authored with Ron Marken; they turned their book, **1919: The Love Letters of George and Adelaide**, into a play, *Dancing In Poppies*, which was produced by The Globe Theatre of Regina in 1993.

Gail turned to writing mystery stories in 1985 because she enjoyed reading them. "Murder mysteries do not glorify violence," she explains. "I don't think the good ones are ever casual about violence, either. It's always seen as a clear violation of the order that should be there. Most often, (in murder mysteries) evil in punished".

Her first mystery, **Deadly Appearances** (Douglas & McIntyre, 1990) was inspired by a New Democratic Party picnic she attended in 1989. Looking at all the party faithful gathered around leader Roy Romanow, she reflected on how good it was to live in a country where political assassinations are virtually unheard of. The thought evolved into the story of Joanne Kilbourn, a widowed political speech writer who investigates the murder of her boss. **Deadly Appearances** was a finalist in the 1990 W.H. Smith Books in Canada Best First Novel Contest.

A second Joanne Kilbourn mystery was published in the fall of 1991. **Murder at the Mendel**, (published in the U.S. as **Love and Murder**) is an examination of family ties and wilful egos in the art world. Gail Bowen followed **Mendel** with **The Wandering Soul Murders** (Douglas & McIntyre, 1992; St. Martins Press, 1994) which takes Joanne Kilbourn into the world of street kids and prostitutes and the people who exploit them. A fourth Joanne Kilbourn novel, **The Ian Kilbourn Case** will be published by McClelland and Stewart in 1994.

Gail Bowen's adaptation of *Beauty and the Beast* was the Globe Theatre's Christmas production in 1993, and she has been commissioned to write the Globe's 1994 Christmas show.

Festival 9 (1991) & Workshop Spring 1992

CHICKEN LIVER PATE

As described in her novel **Deadly Appearances.**

1/4 cup **butter**
1 lb **chicken livers**
1/2 cup finely chopped **onion**
1 tsp **salt**
1/4 tsp **dry mustard**

1/4 tsp **freshly ground black pepper**
1/4 tsp **powdered thyme**
1/8 tsp **mace**
1/4 cup **cream**

- Heat butter in skillet. Add chicken livers and onions; cook over medium heat, stirring until livers are done and onions are tender.
- Put above mixture into blender or food processor. Blend until smooth. Add seasonings and cream. Turn into a mold and leave until set.

POPPY SEED CHEESECAKE

CRUST

1 cup **flour**
3 tbsp **sugar**
1/4 tsp **salt**

1/2 cup **butter**
1 **egg yolk**
1 tbsp **cream**

- Rub flour, sugar, salt and butter together in a bowl.
- Beat the egg yolk with the cream and add to crumb mixture
- Press in buttered 9" x 9" pan (or 9" springform).
- Bake at 350°F for 25 minutes. Cool.

FILLING

12 oz **cream cheese**
1 1/2 tsp **vanilla**

2 **eggs**
1/2 cup **sugar**

- Beat eggs with sugar.
- Combine with other ingredients and whip until smooth.
- Pour over crust.
- Bake at 350°F for 25 minutes.
- Cool 15 minutes.

POPPYSEED LAYER

1 cup **poppy seeds**
3/4 cup soaked & drained **raisins**
3/4 cup **sugar**

1/2 cup **milk**
2 1/2 tsp **lemon rind**
1/2 tsp **vanilla**

- Combine all ingredients except vanilla in saucepan and cook for 10 minutes.
- Stir in vanilla.
- Cool. Spoon over cheesecake.

STREUSEL TOPPING

1/3 cup **brown sugar**
1/3 cup **flour**
2 tbsp **butter**

- Rub ingredients together.
- Sprinkle over poppy seed mixture.
- Bake at 350°F for 15 minutes.
- Chill.

LYNNE BOWEN

Nanaimo historian Lynne Bowen was born in Indian Head, Saskatchewan, raised in Alberta and trained as a public health nurse at the University of Alberta. After moving to British Columbia, she studied Western Canadian History at the University of Victoria, receiving her M.A. in 1980.

Her desire to demonstrate to a general readership that Canada has a history worth telling found a perfect outlet when a group of retired coal miners asked her to write a book based on their extensive collection of tape recorded memories. **Boss Whistle: The Coal Miners of Vancouver Island Remember** (Oolichan Books) won the Eaton's B.C. Book Award in 1983 and subsequently was awarded a Canadian Historical Association Regional Certificate of Merit. **Three Dollar Dreams** (Oolichan Books), which followed in 1987, covered the earlier years of the miners' story from 1848 to 1900. The book received the Lieutenant Governor's Medal for best book on B.C. history, but the author admitted still feeling "like a revolutionary, part of a growing number of Canadian history writers who are fighting for and winning over an audience schooled on the BNA Act and entertained with movies and books about American cowboys and British kings."

After spending ten years explaining that she was not a coal miner's daughter, Lynne Bowen welcomed the chance to write a story in which her own family took part. **Muddling Through: The Remarkable Story of the Barr Colonists** (Douglas & McIntyre) won the Hubert Evans Non-Fiction Prize in the 1993 B.C. Book Awards and the Canadian Historical Association Regional Certificate of Merit for the Prairies and Northwest Territories. Working with an extensive collection of memoirs and diaries, Lynne pieced the story together, discovering in the process the occasional family skeleton.

Lynne Bowen is a Maclean Hunter lecturer in the University of British Columbia's Creative Writing Department. She loves recipe books.

Festival 6 (1988)

EDMONTON BUTTER TARTS

(These made me the woman I am today, alas!)

Pastry for eight tarts
1 cup **Sultana raisins**
1 cup **brown sugar**

1 **egg**
1/2 tsp **vanilla**
ice cream

- Preheat oven to 400°F.
- Line eight of the depressions in a large muffin pan with your favorite pastry.
- Soak 1 cup Sultana raisins in boiling water for five minutes and then drain.
- In a small bowl mix the raisins, 1 cup brown sugar, and 1 beaten egg and beat for as long as you can. (The woman who gave me this recipe said, "Beat for five minutes," but I've never been able to do that.)
- Add 1/2 tsp vanilla.
- Fill pastry shells with the mixture and bake 20 minutes.
- Serve warm with ice cream.

TURKEY CARCASS SOUP

(With bows to Janet Berton and Jane Brody)

1 **large turkey carcass**
12 cups **cold water**
1 **large onion,** chopped
1 **celery stalk,** diced
2 **medium carrots,** chopped

1/2 tsp **savory**
1/4 tsp **thyme**
1/4 tsp **garlic salt or powder**
1/4 tsp **pepper**

2 tbsp minced **onion**
1 clove minced **garlic**
1 tbsp **oil**
1 cup diced **carrots**
1/2 cup diced **celery**
1/2 cup finely chopped **mushrooms**

1 1/2 tbsp **flour**
1 tsp **marjoram**
salt and pepper
1/3 cup **raw barley or rice**
2 cups cubed **leftover turkey meat**
a dash **Tabasco**

- Place first nine ingredients in a large Dutch oven. Bring to a boil and reduce heat; simmer for 2 1/2 hours.
- Place a large colander over a very large bowl and pour the contents of the Dutch oven into the colander to strain the solids from the broth. Discard the solids and place the large bowl of broth in a cold place for several hours or overnight to allow the fat to solidify on top. Skim off the fat and discard.

(Continued on pg. 28)

About 1 1/2 hours before the meal:
• Saute onion and garlic in oil in a large saucepan until soft.
• Add carrots, celery, and mushrooms, and cook, stirring, for 3 to 5 minutes longer.
• Add flour and cook the mixture, stirring, for another minute.
• Add 6 - 7 cups of the turkey broth and bring to a boil.
• Add marjoram, salt, pepper, barley or rice.
• Adjust seasonings.
• Add turkey meat and tabasco and heat to boiling.
• Sprinkle the soup with finely chopped parsley just before serving.

SHARON BUTALA

When Sharon Butala spoke at the Festival of the Written Arts in 1984, she had only been writing for six years, but in that time, she had published three poems, six pieces of non-fiction, nine pieces of short fiction and a novel, and won five writing awards.

Born, raised and educated in Saskatchewan, Sharon Butala taught high school English and worked with mentally handicapped and learning disabled children before she began her writing career. She prepared by taking workshops with W.D. Valgardson and Jack Hodgins. Although she planned to be a novelist, she began by publishing short stories in periodicals such as *Western People*, *Grain* and *NeWest Review*.

Her first novel, **Country Of The Heart** was published by Fifth House in 1984. Her first short story collection, **Queen of the Headaches** (1985), was shortlisted for the Governor General's Award. It was followed by **Upstream/ Le Pays d'en Haut** (Fifth House), a timely story of the dual cultural realities that confront a French/English woman in Saskatchewan exploring her past in the face of the unravelling of her present life. Sharon Butala's next work, the loosely linked trilogy of novels: **Luna, The Gates of the Sun** and **The Fourth Archangel** (HarperCollins, 1992), brought acclaim from reviewers. Of the final volume, the *Globe and Mail's* John Moss wrote "Nowhere has the small town in Canada been brought better into narrative focus— even, paradoxically, as it fades from existence."

Sharon Butala's essay **Harvest: A Celebration of Harvest on the Canadian Prairies**, illustrated by the photographs of Todd Korol, follows the Peters family who farm near Hanley, Saskatchewan. Her short stories were collected in **Fever** published by HarperCollins in 1990; it was nominated for the 1991 Commonwealth Award and received the 1992 Authors Award for Paperback Fiction. In February 1994 her first work of non-fiction, **The Perfection of the Morning: An Apprenticeship in Nature**, about her 18 years on a Saskatchewan ranch, was released by HarperCollins.

Festival 2 (1984)

Okay, here goes! My favourite dessert, first:

CREME CARAMEL

1 cup **sugar**	1 tsp **vanilla**
2 **eggs**	pinch **salt**
2 cups **light cream**	

- Caramelize half a cup of the sugar and coat the inside of a mold with it. You can use more sugar if you like more caramel sauce. You caramelize it by putting the sugar in the bottom of a heavy pan at medium high and shaking it to keep it from burning. Watch it very closely because it burns easily. The sugar melts to liquid and turns brown.
- Heat the light cream till tiny bubbles appear around the edge.
- In the meantime beat slightly two eggs, add the other half cup of sugar, vanilla and salt, and mix together.
- Add the hot cream slowly to the egg mixture and mix.
- Pour into the mold which has been coated with the caramelized sugar.
- Place the mold in a pan of hot water and set in a 350°F oven until a silver knife inserted in the centre comes out clean (about 35 minutes).
- Cool for about six hours or overnight. Unmold. If the dessert isn't sufficiently chilled, it won't unmold. This recipe serves 4 - 5, but it can be doubled.

CREAM OF BROCCOLI SOUP

This is a vegetable soup which can be made in under half an hour and is fairly hearty—I cook for hard-working men every day—and yet it is elegant.

3 cups **water**	3 tbsp **flour**
3 **chicken OXO cubes**	2 cups or more of chopped **broccoli with**
1/2 cup finely chopped **onion**	**some flowerets carefully kept whole**
1/2 cup finely chopped **celery**	1 cup **whole milk**
3 tbsp **butter**	**salt & pepper** to taste

- In a pot heat the water, dissolve the chicken flavour cubes in it, and add the broccoli. Simmer till the broccoli is tender, but not soft.
- In a smaller pot melt the butter, saute the chopped onion and celery in the butter till the onion is translucent, then stir in the flour. Cook the mixture for a couple of minutes till it thickens.
- Stir the milk in bit by bit to avoid lumps. Heat till the mixture thickens and bubbles.
- Just before serving, add the flour mixture carefully to the hot chicken and broccoli mixture and add the seasonings.
- Some cooks might choose to put half the soup in the blender and then return it to the soup pot, for a creamier, greenish-coloured soup.

NICOLA CAVENDISH

Nicola Cavendish's writing career, which she describes as "the only thing I *really* want to do", has had to take second place to one of the busiest acting careers in Canadian theatre. Illustrative of the schedule that she keeps, the incredibly versatile Ms. Cavendish came to the 10th Festival of the Written Arts from a tour of Manitoba and Ontario with the play **Shirley Valentine** for which she won both a Jessie and a Dora Award. She followed her appearance in Sechelt with a performance of Shaw's **Millionairess** in Vancouver, then returned to **Shirley Valentine** for November in Ottawa, then back to Vancouver for December.

In her 18-year career in theatre she has become a regular at Vancouver's Arts Club and Playhouse Theatres and in Ontario at the Shaw Festival, and has performed in principal roles at the National Arts Centre, the Manitoba Theatre Centre, Toronto's Canadian Stage, and toured Calgary, Victoria, Winnipeg, Toronto and many other cities. She appeared at the Neil Simon Theatre on Broadway in **Blithe Spirit** with Richard Chamberlain and Geraldine Page. Between stage shows she has amassed television and film credits, including her roles in **Angel Square**, Anne Wheeler's adaptation of **The Diviners**, John Pozer's film **The Grocer's Wife** for which she won a Genie and Sandy Wilson's **My American Cousin**.

This acclaimed actress is also the playwright who wrote **North Shore Live**, a satire on television, the enormously successful stage play **Snowing on Saltspring**, and the 1992 hit **It's Blowin' on Bowen**. She has a new play in progress: **Winter Windows**, which explores the life of the Ontario pioneer woman, Catherine Parr Trail.

Festival 10 (1992)

WILD RICE SOUP (By way of the Premier of Manitoba's kitchen)

1 cup **wild rice**
2 qts **chicken broth**
1/4 to 1/2 cup **butter**
1/2 cup **celery,** diced
1 cup **onion,** chopped
1/2 cup **carrot,** grated
1/2 to 1 cup **flour**

1/2 to 1 cup **ham**
   (**smoked Black Forest** is best)
4 cups **light cream**
1/2 cup **slivered almonds,** toasted
1/2 tsp **salt**
pepper

- Put rice in sieve and wash under cold water.
- Boil 3 cups water. Stir in rice.
- Parboil five minutes covered.
- Remove from heat and let stand covered one hour. Drain.
- Add chicken stock. Cook covered for 45 minutes on medium heat.
- In frypan, saute vegetables in butter till soft. Add flour. Stir and cook 3 minutes. Add vegetables to rice mixture. Blend.
- Just prior to serving, add cream and ham. Season to taste. Sprinkle almonds on top.

For reduced calories and lower fat:
- Reduce butter to 1/4 cup.
- Reduce flour to 1/2 cup.
- Use skim milk instead of cream.

This sustains me when I am living out of a suitcase in a hotel on the road again!

MRS. SEMPLE'S PERFECT FUDGE

My Best Friend's Mom's Bestest Fudge!

3 small pkts **pure chocolate chips**
1/2 cup **butter**
4 1/2 cups! **white sugar**

1 can **Carnation milk**
3 tbsp **vanilla**

- Put chocolate, butter and vanilla in a big bowl.
- Boil sugar and milk for six minutes from a rolling boil.
- Pour into bowl and mix well, fast.
- Pour onto wax paper lined cookie sheet.
- Cut before it hardens, then break it into pieces.

One small piece of this fudge sends this diabetic into heaven!

LORNA CROZIER

Acknowledged as one of the best poets writing in Canada today, especially in her articulation of the female experience—and particularly the sexual element of that experience, Lorna Crozier writes poetry that is witty, provocative and wonderfully accessible. In fact, Margaret Laurence described her as "a poet to be grateful for".

Ms. Crozier published her first book of poetry, **Inside is the Sky** (Thistledown) in 1976, and followed it with seven more collections: **Crow's Black Joy** (NeWest Press, 1979), **Humans and Other Beasts** (Turnstone, 1981), **No Longer Two People** (with Patrick Lane; Turnstone, 1981), **The Weather** (Coteau Books, 1983), **The Garden Going On Without Us** (McClelland & Stewart, 1985) **Angels of Flesh, Angels of Silence** (M & S, 1988), and **Inventing the Hawk** (M & S, 1992).

The Weather, Crow's Black Joy, and a section of **Angels of Flesh, Angels of Silence** were winners of Saskatchewan poetry manuscript awards. While both **The Garden Going On Without Us** and **Angels of Flesh, Angels of Silence** had been nominated for the Governor General's Poetry Award, Lorna Crozier won the award for **Inventing the Hawk** in 1992. This collection also received the Canadian Authors' Association Award for poetry and the League of Canadian Poets' Pat Lowther Award.

Her poetry has been published in magazines in Canada and the U.S., including *Saturday Night*, *The Malahat Review*, *Fiddlehead* and *Descant* and in such anthologies as *The Oxford Anthology of Canadian Literature in English*, *The New Canadian Poets* (McClelland & Stewart), *Twenty Poets for the Eighties* (Anansi), and *Anything is Possible* (Mosaic). Lorna Crozier has taught creative writing at the Banff School of Fine Arts, the Sage Hill Writing Experience, the Red Deer College Writers on Campus Program and the Writers-in-Residence Program in Sechelt. She has also been Writer-in-Residence at the University of Toronto, and now teaches in the Creative Writing Department of the University of Victoria.

Festival 10 (1992) & Workshop 1988

MARY'S CORN SOUP

I love recipes that are named after friends. Every time I make this soup I think of Mary who now lives 1,000 miles away.

1/4 lb boned **white chicken meat** (I use a whole chicken breast.)
1 can **creamed corn**
1/2 tsp **cornstarch** mixed with 1 tbsp **water**
2 tsp **curry powder** (adjust to taste)
1 **egg white,** beaten
1 cup **chicken stock**

- If using cooked chicken, mince finely. If using raw chicken, slice it into bite-size pieces, and fry it in a small amount of butter.
- Place chicken in a medium saucepan and add corn and chicken stock.
- Bring to boil and thicken with cornstarch mixture.
- Remove from heat and stir in beaten egg white.

MYRTLE'S GINGER SNAPS

This recipe was given to me by Myrtle who lived upstairs in a rented suite in the house where I grew up.

1 cup **white sugar**
3/4 cup **margarine**
1 **egg,** beaten
1 tsp **ground ginger**
1 tsp **cinnamon**

1 tsp **cloves**
2 cups **flour**
2 tsp **baking soda**
4 tbsp **molasses**

- Mix in order given.
- Form into balls and dip one side in sugar.
- Place on an ungreased pan, sugar side up, allowing room to spread.
- Bake 15 min in a 350°F oven.

PHILIP J. CURRIE

Recognized internationally as one of the world's foremost dinosaurian palaeontologists, Dr. Philip J. Currie is the author of **The Flying Dinosaurs: The Illustrated Guide to the Evolution of Flight** (1992), a step by step explanation of his theory of the slow evolution of today's birds from the carnivorous or theropod dinosaurs. The process of linking the two has been controversial because fossils of primitive birds with wings and feathers intact have rarely been found. Dr. Currie has also written more than 45 scientific and 40 popular publications focussed primarily on growth and variation of extinct reptiles, the anatomy and relationships of carnivorous dinosaurs and the origin of birds. The fieldwork connected with his research in these areas has been concentrated in Alberta, British Columbia, the Arctic and China.

As Adjunct Associate Professor at the University of Calgary, Dr. Currie supervises graduate student work in palaeontology, but he also manages the Dinosaur Research Program at the world renowned Royal Tyrrell Museum of Palaeontology at Drumheller in the heart of the Alberta badlands. Here he and his students are investigating some of the finest examples of prehistoric life known in the world.

Dr. Currie is also co-leader of the Canada-China Dinosaur Project, the largest dinosaur exploration ever undertaken. He has conducted field research in many other parts of the world, and lectured throughout North America, Europe, Australia and Asia on dinosaur evolution. In 1992 Dr. Currie's work was extensively documented on the American Public Broadcasting System's *Nova* series.

In 1988 he received the Sir Frederick Haultain Award for significant contributions to science in Alberta. A new book on dinosaurs which he co-authored with Z. Spinar will be published in 1994 in English, Czech, German, Polish and Spanish. Another new book will be published in Japanese in Japan.

Festival 10 (1992)

SMOKED COD AU GRATIN

This fish recipe is something I periodically throw together, and because there is no actual recipe (or wasn't until I wrote it down) it never turns out quite the same. The quantities are approximations; I usually add a sprinkle of this and that, and just cook it until it is done. I also vary the spices somewhat.

2 lbs **smoked Cod** 1 kg
28 oz can **tomatoes,** cut up 800 ml
(or use 5 medium **fresh tomatoes**)
1 med **onion,** chopped
2 cloves **garlic,** crushed or chopped
3 sprigs **parsley,** chopped

1/2 tsp **basil**
1/2 tsp **pepper or to taste**
1/2 tsp **tarragon**
1/4 cup **almonds,** slivered
2 cups **old cheddar cheese,**
    grated parmesan cheese

- Soak smoked cod in water for 3 hours.
- Debone and cut into 2 centimeter cubes and layer in bottom of 9 x 12 baking dish.
- Drain and add tomatoes, chopped onions, garlic.
- Bake in 400°F oven for 10 minutes.
- Drain excess liquid, and add parsley, basil, pepper and tarragon.
- Bake a further fifteen minutes.
- Stir in slivered almonds.
- Layer cheddar cheese on top and sprinkle with parmesan.
- Return to oven until cheese is melted.

MICROWAVE METHOD
- Microwave fish, tomatoes, onions and garlic on high power for 7 minutes. Drain.
- Add herbs and spices.
- Microwave on high for 10 minutes.
- Stir in almonds and spread cheese on top.
- Sprinkle with parmesan.
- Cover with wax paper.
- Microwave for 1 minute at medium power or until cheese is melted.

Serving: 4 or 5 people. Serve on bed of rice, with vegetable on side.

POACHED EGGS

Eggs
Butter or margarine
Cheddar cheese - cut into 2 centimeter long sticks
Basil
Pepper

- A double level egg poacher with individual egg cups is necessary for this recipe.
- Bring water to boil.
- Add quarter teaspoon of butter to each cup. Rotate cup until melted butter coats inside.
- Add pinch of basil and pinch of pepper to each cup, then the egg.
- Push cheese sticks into egg white around the yolk.
- Cook to taste. Serve on English muffins.

EDITH IGLAUER  DALY

Internationally known freelance journalist Edith Iglauer Daly's career began in New York writing $10 articles for the *Christian Science Monitor*. During World War II she married journalist Philip Hamburger, then travelled with him to postwar Belgrade where she served as correspondent for the Cleveland *News*. Returning to New York, she began writing for *Harpers* and the *New Yorker* as well as most of the other important journals in the U.S. Her book **Seven Stones** (Harbour, 1981) was an enlargement of a 1979 *New Yorker* profile on Vancouver architect Arthur Erickson.

In 1959, having attended the first showing of Inuit carvings in New York City, she persuaded *New Yorker* editor Bill Shawn to send her to Ungava Bay in northern Quebec to report on the first Inuit co-operative. The four articles that she wrote on the Inuit were the basis of her first book, **The New People**, published in 1966 and re-issued as **Inuit Journey** in 1979. Later trips to Canada's north resulted in **Denison's Ice Road** (1974, re-issued by Harbour, 1991); it is the story of the construction of a 520 kilometer ice road between Yellowknife and Great Bear Lake.

Edith Iglauer came to live on British Columbia's west coast in 1974 and soon afterwards married fisherman John Daly. Their blissful marriage ended with his death of a heart attack four years later, and after a hiatus of nearly two years in which she wrote nothing, she began to put on paper her memories of her life with him aboard his boat the *MoreKelp*. The story appeared first as an article for the *New Yorker*, then was expanded into the book **Fishing with John** which was nominated for the 1989 Governor General's Award.

The Strangers Next Door (Harbour, 1991) is a 50-year retrospective anthology of her work from the 1940s when she covered Eleanor Roosevelt's press conferences, through to the 1980s when she bestowed some of her best writing on British Columbia subjects such as artist Bill Reid and novelist Hubert Evans. The book takes its title from a 1973 study that she wrote about Canadians for the American readers of the *Atlantic Monthly*.

Festival 2 (1984)

HAZELNUT TORTE

This cake is made in a blender; the icing is made in the food processor.

4 **eggs**
3/4 cup **white sugar**
2 tbsp **flour**

2 1/2 tsp **baking powder**
1 cup **ground hazelnuts (or filberts)**

- In blender, whirl the eggs and sugar until mixed.
- Add flour, baking powder and hazelnuts.
- Blend at high speed.
- Pour into greased 8-inch layer pan.
- Bake at 350°F for 20 - 30 minutes, until done.

ICING:

1/4 cup **soft butter**
1 1/2 cups **icing sugar**

4 tsp **cocoa**
1 tbsp **rum**

- Cream butter and icing sugar in food processor.
- Add cocoa and rum.

To make a good sized Hazelnut layer cake, I make the recipe twice, using two 8-inch pans. I add a thin layer of preserves or jam, preferably raspberry, on top of cocoa icing in the middle, and decorate the top with an edge of ground nuts.

CORN PUDDING

This was my mother's recipe, to which I have added other ingredients. I come from Ohio, which is corn country.

1 can **niblet corn or 6 ears of corn cut off the cob**. I like Mexicorn because it has some pimento and green pepper in it, which add colour.
3 **eggs**
1 cup **milk**
1 big lump **butter**, melted (Can use margarine)
1 tbsp **flour**
salt & pepper to taste
paprika

OPTIONAL:

dash Tabasco
small onion, chopped
red and/or green pepper, chopped
parsley, chopped

dill, chopped
basil, chopped
tarragon (which I grow), chopped

- Have a buttered baking dish ready.
- Beat eggs, add milk and corn. Mix.
- Add flour, butter, Tabasco, fresh ground pepper (I don't use salt), any fresh or dried herbs you want.
- Pour mixture into a baking dish. Sprinkle with paprika.
- Bake 375° F in a pan of water for one hour.

Note: This is such a simple recipe, that I mix the whole thing in the Cuisinart, which chops up the onion and herbs and beats the eggs, all at once. Another advantage—if dinner is late, it just sits in its hot bath and turns a little browner on the top but doesn't dry up.

SARAH ELLIS

Sarah Ellis was born in Vancouver and although she has travelled and lived elsewhere she always misses the sea and has to come home. "As a child I read everything in sight" she says, "and when I grew up I was lucky enough to find a career where reading is allowed." During her ten years as a children's librarian she discovered a delight in performing, in puppetry and story-telling. Her interest in writing about children's books led her to spend a year at the Center for the Study of Children's Literature at Simmons College, Boston. She now writes a column on Canadian children's literature for the American review magazine *The Hornbook* and sometimes teaches courses in children's literature.

It was almost inevitable that having had this much pleasure from children's books, she would one day try her hand at writing juvenile fiction herself. **The Baby Project** (Canada: Groundwood, 1986; U.S.: Macmillan) was the result. It won the B.C. Book Prizes Sheila Egoff Award, earned a place on the *Hornbook* Fanfare List, and was named an American Library Association Notable Children's Book. Her second book for children, **Next-Door Neighbours** (Canada: Groundwood, 1989; U.S.: Macmillan), was runner-up for the Sheila Egoff Award and for the City of Vancouver

Book Award. It became a Junior Library Guild selection and was chosen for the *School Library Journal* Best Books of 1990 list.

Pick-Up Sticks (Canada: Groundwood, 1991; U.S.: Macmillan, 1992), her latest novel for children, won the Governor General's Award for Children's Literature, was short-listed for the Mr. Christie Book Award and was runner-up for the Sheila Egoff Award. She has also written the text for a picture book, **Putting Up With Mitchell**, illustrated by Barbara Wood and published by Brighouse Press in 1989; it was runner-up for the City of Vancouver Book Award. Her two storytelling tapes, produced with friend Bill Richardson, are called **Pobbles and Porridge Pots** and **Mud and Gold** (First Avenue Press, 1986).

Sarah has given readings in schools and libraries all across Canada. She is currently at work on **Staying Inside the Lines** which will be published by Groundwood in the fall of 1994.

Festival 5 (1987)

EGGPLANT DIP

This is one of those recipes that is more than the sum of its parts. It has a great smooth consistency and a smoky afterglow. Good with raw veggies or wedges of pita bread.

2 **eggplants**
oil
3 tbsp **olive oil**
2 tbsp **parsley,** chopped

1 clove **garlic,** crushed
juice of one **lemon**
salt and pepper

- Take a couple of eggplants, cut them in half, brush oil over the cut surface, and put them, cut side down, on a cookiesheet. Then broil the heck out of them, until they are black and blistery on the outside.
- Spoon out the flesh, now soft and juicy, into a food processor.
- While the eggplant is blurring around, add olive oil.
- Add parsley, garlic clove, lemon, salt and pepper.

AUTUMN SOUP

I made up this recipe so I don't have exact quantities. But soups are very forgiving. The only hard part is peeling the chestnuts. I've read various methods for peeling baked chestnuts, but in my experience none of them work. Therefore, I would advise all but the purists to use a can of chestnut puree.

1 pot **turkey broth**
2 **carrots**
1 can **pureed chestnuts**
onions, sliced

garlic
salt & pepper
1/2 cup **orange juice**
light cream

- Take a pot of turkey broth. Slice a couple of carrots and cook them in aforesaid broth until they are tender.
- Add pureed chestnuts.
- Saute some onions and garlic and add that to the pot.
- Puree the whole mixture in a food processor and then put it back into the pot.
- Add salt, pepper, about half a cup of orange juice and some light cream.
- Heat it up but don't boil it.

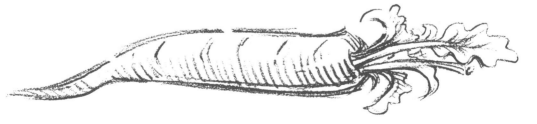

CYNTHIA FLOOD

Cynthia Flood's short fiction has appeared in a wide range of Canadian magazines—generalist, feminist, literary, socialist. Her work has been frequently anthologized, most recently in **Streets of Attitude** (winner of the City of Toronto Prize in 1991), and in **Canadian Short Stories: Fifth Series**, edited by Robert Weaver. Her stories have also been read on various CBC programs, and one was included in the feature film *Martha, Ruth, and Edie*, directed by Deepa Mehta in 1988.

The Animals in their Elements, her first collection of stories, appeared in 1987, followed by **My Father Took a Cake to France** in 1992 (both Talonbooks). The title story of the latter won The Journey Prize in 1991, and the book itself has received high praise from reviewers across the country. Currently she is at work on a linked sequence of stories, **A Civil Plantation**; set in the 1950s in England and Canada, these stories treat the parallel themes of colonialism and adult control over the young.

Since the 1970s, Cynthia Flood has taught English at Langara College in Vancouver, where she is active in the faculty union and was among the founders of a Women's Studies program now celebrating its twentieth anniversary. She has long been a participant in the women's movement, the left and—in recent years—in writers' organizations.

Workshops Summer 1992

BEST PANCAKES

1 cup **whole wheat flour**
1 cup **cake/pastry flour**
2 tsp **sugar**
1 1/2 tsp **baking powder**

1 tsp **baking soda**
2 **eggs**
2 cups **buttermilk or yogurt**

- Combine dry ingredients.
- Combine wet ingredients.
- Combine the two.
- Don't beat batter smooth—some lumpiness is good.

PLUM CRISP

plums, pitted and quartered (enough for a buttered 9x9 or 10x10 baking dish).

1/2 cup **rolled oats**
1/3 cup **flour**
1/2 cup **brown sugar**
dash **salt**

1/2 tsp **nutmeg**
1/3 cup **butter,** very soft
1/3 cup **almonds,** chopped

- Place plums in buttered baking dish.
- Mix the next seven ingredients and distribute over the fruit.
- Bake at 350°F for half an hour or so, till the topping is brown and the purple juice bubbles up at the edges.

QUICK VEG DINNER

This is my ideal home-alone dinner. With luck, there will be some leftover rice or noodles to go with the vegetables.

assorted vegetables, cut up
sesame oil for stir fry

2 tbsp **tahini,** or to taste
1 tbsp **tamari,** or to taste

- Cut up enough vegetables to feed yourself—whatever you like best or are trying to clear out of the fridge or both. Many are good: mushrooms, zucchini, carrots, scallions, celery, bok choy, garlic, turnip, sprouts, cherry tomatoes, red pepper, cabbage, snow peas, wax beans. Bits of tofu and leftover cooked potatoes are good too.
- Stir fry these vegetables in sesame oil. When they are almost done, add a couple of tablespoons of tahini and a good slosh of tamari.
- Stir hard, and there's dinner.

DENNIS FOON

Dennis Foon is one of Canada's leading writers of theatre, television and film for young audiences. A co-founder, in 1975, of Green Thumb Theatre, he was its artistic director for 12 years, where he directed, wrote or dramaturged many award-winning productions.

His own plays have been produced extensively throughout Canada and the world, translated into French, Danish, Hebrew and Cantonese. They include **New Canadian Kid** and **Invisible Kids** (published by Pulp Press, 1989), which he staged at the Unicorn Theatre in London, England in 1985 and subsequently won the British Theatre Award. His play about teens and racism in Canada, **Skin** (published by Playwrights Canada, 1988), won the Chalmers Award and was nominated for the Governor General's Award in Drama.

His plays **Seesaw** (about children and aggression) and **Mirror Game** (examining family violence) were both published by Blizzard (1993 and 1992 respectively) and have been seen all over North America. His latest play, **The Short Tree And The Bird That Could Not Sing**, is an adaptation of his 1985 CBC Literary Award-winning children's picture book (Groundwood, 1986).

Dennis received the International Arts for Young Audiences Award in 1989 for his outstanding contribution in the field of arts for young people, and in 1990 he received the Scott Newman Award.

Festival 4 (1986)

FAST AND DUMB CLAM SAUCE

6-8 **whole cloves of garlic,** peeled
10 oz can **clams**
28 oz can **tomatoes,** chopped, or **tomato sauce,** or **fresh tomatoes** with skin removed.
1 tbsp **olive oil**

- Brown the whole garlic cloves in the olive oil.
- Add the clam broth from the can.
- Cover. Simmer for 5 minutes.
- Moosh the garlic cloves with a fork.
- Add tomatoes (or sauce). If using fresh tomatoes, simmer for about 10 minutes until they're cooked down.
- Add clams and let sauce simmer a couple of minutes.
- Serve over the pasta of your choice.
- Serves two or three.

MEAN SALAD

3-4 medium to large **tomatoes,** sliced and quartered
1 medium size head of **Romaine lettuce**
4 tsp **capers** (heaping tsps)

THE DRESSING
2 tbsp **balsamic vinegar**
1 tbsp **olive oil**
1 tsp **mustard seeds,** crushed
3-4 **garlic cloves,** diced and crushed

- Mix the dressing ingredients together in a jar and shake well. This stuff keeps well in the fridge, so feel free to make a large batch and vary the ingredients to taste.
- Wash and dry the lettuce leaves, then tear into edible pieces.
- Throw into bowl. Add tomatoes.
- Roughly mix with the dressing. You want to bruise the leaves a bit and get some of the tomato seeds and juice to mix into the vinegar, so don't be gentle.
- Plop onto plates.
- Sprinkle daintily with capers (to taste).

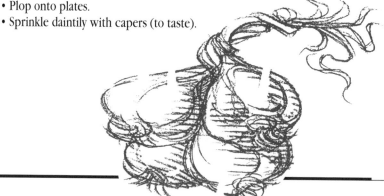

JOE GARNER

Ex-logger, ex-bush-pilot, ex-construction man Joe Garner's very first book, **Never Fly Over An Eagle's Nest** (1981), sold over 50,000 copies to become a Canadian best seller. The story of his early life, it reveals that this B.C. pioneer was born in a dirt-floored cabin on Saltspring Island in 1909 and started work in the logging industry at the age of 10. "We grew up early in those days," Joe Garner says. "We learned very fast."

His second book, **Never A Time To Trust** (1984) deals with the elusive cougar in its last hunting grounds on the rugged islands and coastal areas of British Columbia.

In 1988, at the age of 80, he produced—and self-published under his Cinnabar Press imprint—his third book, **Never Chop Your Rope**, a collection of linked biographies of key participants in the building of B.C.'s logging industry, a narrative covering most of his eighty years. The title comes from a 1920 incident involving a logger who accidentally chopped through his climbing rope and plunged 40 feet to the ground—and lived. **Never Chop Your Rope** topped the B.C. best seller list for weeks.

His most recent book, **Never Under the Table**, tells the story of the general mismanagement of British Columbia's forests. But more importantly, in it Joe sets out his hopes and recommend-ations for the future of our forest industry.

At eighty-five years of age, Joe Garner maintains the lifestyle he established growing up in British Columbia. He still lives in a log house (although this one has a proper floor), remains an avid outdoorsman and a reader. He often lectures to forestry, museum and history groups.

Joe Garner is currently writing what he says will be his last book. Under the working title of **Never Forget the Good Times**, his personal memoirs are scheduled for completion later this year.

Festival 7 (1989)

VENISON ROAST

For those who can wait two or three days, this dish is worth the wait.
Cut a 4 to 5 lb roast of venison and remove the bone.

MARINADE:

1/2 cup **red wine vinegar**
1 cup **water**
1/2 cup **salad oil**
1 large **clove garlic**, cut in half

1 tsp **rosemary (or 1/2 tsp thyme)**
1 **bay leaf**
salt and pepper

- Put the venison in a deep pan with marinade and let stand two to three days in the refrigerator, turning several times.
- Put meat in a roaster and cover it with slices of well smoked fatty bacon. Cook covered in moderate oven (350°F) for 45 minutes, basting frequently with a little of the marinade.
- Remove cover and roast for another 1/2 hour. This meat should be medium cooked.
- Remove meat to a warm platter, pour off excess fat and make gravy.

Especially good served with peas and wild rice.

SOUTHERN STYLE SWEET MILK GRAVY WITH GROUSE OR PHEASANT

A quick and delectable meal for anyone, but especially the hunter.

- Skin birds and remove giblets; separate breast, wings and legs. Roll these in flour seasoned with salt and pepper. If you like curry, just add a couple of pinches for a very special flavour.
- In a large cast iron frying pan heat 1/2 cup of butter and fry all the pieces until golden brown. Then add 2 or 3 tablespoons of wine vinegar, cover and cook until tender.
- Remove the larger pieces and keep them warm.
- Now add 2 rounded tablespoons of the remaining seasoned flour and stir over high heat until brown, then add milk slowly until you have the desired consistency. Make sure the milk continues to bubble while you are adding it. Let it simmer for several minutes more, adding extra salt and pepper if necessary.
- Place the larger pieces of meat on heated plates with toasted brown bread or hot rice. Pour the gravy, with the smaller pieces in it, over the toast or rice.

Use YOUNG birds for the best results. Chicken is also delightful when cooked this way.

JUDY GILL

The granddaughter of two Sunshine Coast pioneering families, romance writer Judy Gill was born at the Columbia Coast Mission Hospital in Pender Harbour, B.C., and grew up in the isolated community of Egmont surrounded by family. "When I learned to read," she says, "my best friend became the Open Shelf Library in Victoria."

Judy began her professional writing career in the 1970s while living in Germany with her soldier-husband. She sold six books to British publishers before the Gills returned to Canada and the Sunshine Coast. Here she wrote for a bi-weekly trade newspaper and then managed a bookstore before returning to writing.

"When a friend gave me some Bantam Loveswept books to read," she says, "I recognized that this was exactly the tone that mine have always taken—slightly irreverent, a little bit off the wall, and highly sensual." She adds, "Along with most present day romance writers, I write about the daily lives and loves of women; their relationships with others—lovers, friends and family; exploring topical issues that women need to resolve, and I write about that age-old delight, falling in love. But perhaps most important, I write about hope and like to show that any woman, anywhere, any time, is entitled to that."

Many of Judy's more than two dozen titles have appeared on the U.S. Waldenbooks' bestseller list. *Rendezvous* magazine said of a recent title, "This is incredible reading. Both protagonists are so real you can touch them. A definite must."

Judy is mid-way through a four-book contract with Bantam Doubleday Dell.
Festival 10 (1992)

JUDY GILL'S MAGIC FORMULA FOR DEEP SERENITY

Take one boat, one sunny evening, two or more people, add wine, mix well, and let simmer for an hour or two in a calm, secluded anchorage (preferably in Princess Louisa Inlet). Then throw in a large potful of Nekhani Chowder (see below), enough bowls and spoons to go around, and as many loaves of crusty bread as it takes to fill up the corners.

NEKHANI CHOWDER

A tasty blend of Sunshine Coast seafoods and vegetables, frequently served aboard our little boat, *Nekhani*, with thickly sliced, generously buttered and joyously munched crusty bread, all washed down with plenty of dry white wine.

2 tbsp **vegetable oil**	1 tbsp **fish stock powder**
1 cup chopped **onion**	1 tsp **marjoram**
2 cloves **garlic,** minced	1 tbsp **oregano**
1 - 8 oz can **tomato sauce**	1 tsp **dried basil**
1 - 28 oz can diced **tomatoes**	1 **bay leaf** (optional)
1 can **chicken broth,** diluted	4 **whole cloves** (optional)
2 cans **green beans**	1 lb **boneless cod** fillets
(save liquid from beans)	12 - 15 **raw, peeled prawns**
1/2 cup **white wine or water**	1/2 lb **baby scallops**
1 can **baby clams with nectar**	3 - 4 **clams-in-shell** per person
4 medium **carrots** in chunks	1/4 cup **parsley,** chopped
salt and pepper to taste	

- Saute onion and garlic in oil.
- Add tomatoes, liquids, carrots, canned clams and seasonings except parsley.
- Let simmer 30 minutes or until thick as desired.
- Meanwhile, chop cod into 1" cubes, peel prawns, and scrub clam shells well with a stiff brush.
- Add cod chunks and green beans, simmer further ten minutes. Increase heat until liquid just boiling.
- Add scallops, prawns, clams-in-shell and parsley.
- Cook covered until clam shells open.
- Serve at once, garnishing each bowl with the open clams.

Note: Most of the prep, till just before the addition of the fish, can be done a day ahead, and the results chilled until required.
Note further: This is the Nekhani variation of a basic recipe. Ingredients can be added or deleted as desired. (Variations must be renamed.) Recipe can be doubled, halved, whatever—this one serves four to six.
This chowder may be enjoyed anywhere, but never quite as much as aboard

a boat under the above mentioned conditions. The occasional passing porpoise, eagle, or orca adds relish but is not mandatory. It is possible to make do with nothing more than a pair of fighting kingfishers and a crowd of squalling sea gulls demanding crusts of bread. Try at all costs to avoid crowds of squalling children demanding bites of anything.

SUMPTUOUS FRESH FRUIT SALAD

This fruit salad can be served with fresh whipped cream or ice cream, or just as is. Makes a great finishing touch for any summer meal.

1 **pink grapefruit**	3/4 lb **strawberries**
2 **large oranges**	2 **bananas**
2 **red apples,** skin on	4 **kiwi fruit**
1/2 lb **seedless green grapes**	1/2 cup **Grand Marnier**
1/2 lb **seedless red grapes**	**sugar** to taste
2 **large peaches**	sprinkle of **pumpkin pie spice**

- Peel oranges and grapefruit, break into wedges, cut each wedge in half. Stir together in large mixing bowl.
- Cut apples into wedges, cut each wedge in half; add to citrus fruits.
- Stir gently but well to keep apples from turning brown.
- Sprinkle with sugar if juice not forming.
- Add grapes.
- Peel peaches, cut into wedges similar in size to apples, stir gently into mixture to coat with citrus juices.
- Peel and cut bananas into 1/2" thick coins. Stir gently into mixture.
- Cut strawberries in half, lengthwise, mix in.

Taste juice for sweetness, adding sugar if necessary.
- Remove from mixing bowl, place in clear glass serving dish just barely large enough to hold it.
- Garnish top with peeled, sliced kiwi fruit.
- Drizzle Grand Marnier over, sprinkle on spice, and serve.

Serves 6 - 8

Note: All stirring must be done with a very light hand, so as not to bruise the fruit. The liqueur can be eliminated entirely, or added to individual dishes as preferred.

BRENDA GUILD GILLESPIE

After what she describes as "a twenty-year long, lone apprenticeship in the craft of writing and the art of storytelling, including twelve years research into the tumultuous world of Captain George Vancouver", Coquitlam writer Brenda Guild Gillespie published her first book, **On Stormy Seas: The Triumphs and Torments of Captain George Vancouver** (Horsdal & Schubart, 1992). This creative non-fiction work tells the story of Vancouver's monumental assignment and the faint praise his success garnered on his return to England, as told from the perspective of his elder brother who was responsible for publishing the results of the expedition after the captain's early death.

An Honours Zoology graduate, Brenda Gillespie took her M.Sc. in Education from Simon Fraser University. She has worked as an environmental educator and writer, and in 1975 co-authored (with Patricia Keays) **Encore: A Program of Environmental Studies** for the B.C. government, a work which won first prize for the best nature study program in North America from the American Association for Conservation and Information.

Ms. Gillespie's other publications include both graphic and written work: scenic watercolours and fish illustrations, a series of limited edition fine art prints and contributions to the *Morningside Papers*. She was awarded two prizes from the Nova Scotia Writers Federation for unpublished manuscripts: in 1989 first place for best children's work and in 1990 third place for adult fiction.

Festival 10 (1992)

MELITZANES SALATA
(EGGPLANT SALAD)

Wherever I travelled in Greece, from Thessaloniki (where I worked) to Athens, I ordered this "salad" because its taste varies a great deal, and it's always delicious. No two batches I make are the same either, but it's a hit however it turns out.

2 medium **eggplants**	**parsley**
1 small **onion** chopped	**salt and pepper**
1-2 cloves **garlic,** crushed	1/2 - 1 cup **olive oil**
1/2 tsp **dry mustard**	2 tbsp **lemon juice**
fresh mint	3-4 tbsp **wine vinegar**

- Bake one large or two medium-sized eggplants in the oven at 350-400°F. (I put them in when I'm baking other things, so the temperature is approximate). When they're soft through, remove and cool. (Save them cooked, in the fridge for a few days, if you can't get to them right away.)
- Skin them, cut into messy chunks, and plunk into your blender.

Then add:
- a small, chopped up onion (not too much; I've ruined a batch of this ambrosia with excessive onion);
- a crushed clove or two or three (to taste) of garlic;
- 1/2 tsp of dry mustard (I put this in everything except desserts, to give body to all sorts of flavours);
- fresh mint (lots) and parsley (less); use dried stuff, if that's all you've got;
- salt and pepper;
- 1/2 - 1 cup of olive oil (more equals creamier, but mind your diet, if you must);
- 2 tbsp lemon juice and 3 or 4 tbsp wine vinegar.
- Blend the works until it's a thick, creamy consistency (stop and stir it down as often as necessary). Taste! Is is wonderful yet? No? Try more lemon juice or wine vinegar; add more salt and pepper (remember this is an appetizer, a treat; you can splurge on the salt a little). Tiddle it up, till you can barely resist sampling.
- Store in the fridge in a covered container; it keeps for a week or two. Serve with fresh, warm pita bread, regular bread, or buns. Use torn, bite-sized pieces to scoop it from the communal bowl, Greek style.
- It's also good on rice, pasta and potatoes.
- Encourage hesitant guests to try a very small bite, in the vain hope that they'll dislike it, leaving all the more for you. I've never been so lucky; it vanishes before my eyes, and some who don't know me well actually think I can cook—an undeserved reputation, which I intend never to acquire, or I'll never get away from predatory domesticity and back to reality, which is spinning yarns with my computer.

Our very best family times are spent berry picking in the woods, from huckleberry season in June through blueberries in July to the late Himalayan blackberries of August, and even into cranberry season after the first frost. We sometimes pick with such gusto that we come home with more containers full than we can eat right away—or at all, given that we're stuffed already.

I then get into baking mode (so rare that my children once watched in awe as I made cookies; they didn't know such wonders, outside of store-bought packages, were possible. They invited all their friends to witness the miracle, and they gave away all the spoils. Their dad didn't believe it happened and has never heard such tall tales since.) It was a short-lived insanity brought on by the berry vapours, I guess.

I use a tea cake recipe from my mother-in-law. She makes it with apples, peaches or prunes. I use nature's bounty, and it never fails.

Note: If sloth, rather than inspiration, hits after an intensive berry picking fest, freeze the berries individually on a cookie sheet, then store them in airtight freezer bags. The cake's a bit juicier with thawed berries, but just as good.

WILD BERRY TEA CAKE

1/4 cup **margarine or butter**
1/2 cup **sugar**
2 **eggs**
1/2 tsp **vanilla**
lemon rind

1 1/2 cups **flour**
1 1/2 tsp **baking powder**
1 - 2 cups **berries or peeled, sliced fruit**
extra sugar

- Cream butter. Add sugar.
- Add eggs one at a time. Beat until fluffy.
- Add lemon rind and vanilla.
- Add sifted flour and baking powder.
- Press dough into greased pie plate (with floured fingers).
- Reserve several teaspoons of dough.
- Arrange fruit on top of dough, sprinkle with sugar (more for tart berries). Dot with remaining dough.
- Bake for 35 minutes at 350°F oven.

Deliver steaming hot to the neighbours, with a pint of vanilla ice cream. They, too, will be fooled into thinking you're a kitchen whiz. Tell them it's as easy as pie (whoever said that never made one), knowing full well it's much, much easier, and just as satisfying.

Madness concluded, you can leave them to spread unlikely tales about you, while you get on with what's important—writing, of course, which might include telling even more unlikely stories about them.

L. B. GREENWOOD

L.B. "Beth" Greenwood has always been a great reader, and even as a child found Dickens' work enthralling. So when she began writing, it was natural that she should choose the Victorian period. Her first novel, **The Street Sparrows** (Coward, McCann and Ballantine, 1978) was called "absolutely delightful" by the *Library Journal,* a "rattling good adventure story" by *Kirkus Review*.

Later L.B. Greenwood turned to Sherlock Homes pastiches. She is one of the very few to have received permission from the holder of the copyright to have published three such novels, all well received.

The North American representative said of **The Case of the Raleigh Legacy** (Atheneum and St. Martin's, 1986) that it was "exactly the sort of faithful, straightforward, entertaining Sherlock Holmes mystery that we like to see," and the Vancouver *Sun* remarked that Greenwood has "captured the ambience and texture of the original Conan Doyle work to an extent that is positively uncanny."

The Case of Sabina Hall (Simon and Schuster and Pocket Books, 1988) is set in a snowbound, isolated mansion, that idea coming from Holmes' comment that few people ever learn of crimes done in such places. The *ALA Booklist* said it had "the feel of the real McCoy," *Publishers Weekly* that it was "plausible and twisty" and that "Greenwood's second borrowing from Sir Arthur Conan Doyle tops her first".

The Thistle of Scotland (Simon and Schuster and Pocket Books, 1989) uses a variation on the locked room plot: an heirloom jewel disappears from the hair of an earl's daughter while she is sitting at her wedding breakfast. *Publishers Weekly* called "Greenwood's vivid, authentic evocations of Victorian places, manners and mores" exciting, and *Kirkus Review* said that the story was "refreshingly uncampy and idiosyncratic".

More recently Greenwood has moved to contemporary times for a short story in the anthology **Cold Blood** and novellas in two editions of *Malice Domestic*.

L.B. Greenwood has also given talks and held workshops from coast to coast.
Workshops 1990

THE GREENWOOD CHICKEN STEW

10 **chicken drumsticks**	3/4 can **water**
2 cups **carrots**	3 tbsp **tapioca**
1 cup **celery**	1 tsp **sugar**
4 medium **potatoes**	1 tsp **salt**
1 **onion**	1 tsp **pepper**
1 can **cream of tomato soup**	

- Cut all peeled vegetables into cube size.
- Mix all ingredients together, burying the drumsticks in the vegetables, using a baking dish with a well fitting lid. (As moisture proportions are important with this recipe, I also cover the dish with heavy foil before putting on the lid.)
- Bake at 250° F for five hours. (Yes, those figures are correct.)
- Since ovens and baking dishes have a way of varying a trifle, the first time you try this it's a good idea to take a peek at about the half way time, just to be sure that the heat isn't too much or the moisture too low. The end result should be juicy, very tender and utterly delicious.

For a milder flavour, half a leek can be substituted for the onion.

GRAM'S SWEET RED CABBAGE PICKLE

6 cups **grated red cabbage** (1 small head)	2 cups **water**
3 dessertspoon **table salt**	2 cups **white sugar**
2 cups **white vinegar**	4 dessertspoons **pickling spice**

- Layer the cabbage, two cups at a time, on a large platter and sprinkle each layer with a dessertspoonful of salt. Leave in a cool place for 4 - 5 hours.
- Make syrup of vinegar, water and sugar.
- Cut gauze or other thin material into four squares of about 5". Place 1 dessertspoonful of mixed pickling spice in the centre of each square, gather the material up and tie with white thread to make four small bags.
- Place these in the syrup, bring to a boil, and then simmer for ten minutes.
- Scald four pint jars and tops.
- Rinse the cabbage in cold water and drain well.
- Pack the jars loosely with the cabbage, place a bag of spice in each, fill with the hot syrup, and seal.
- This will be deliciously edible in 2 - 3 weeks.

In our family the syrup is savoured with fried bacon. If this doesn't appeal to your taste, don't waste the syrup: use it to cover sliced canned beets, and again in 2 - 3 weeks you'll have a very tasty pickle.

The darker cabbage makes the prettier pickle, a rich garnet colour. The taste, however, seems the same regardless of the hue of the cabbage used.

KRISTJANA GUNNARS

Icelandic-born Kristjana Gunnars' writing is inspired both by the land of her birth and by the Canadian prairies where she now lives. Her early books of poetry investigated both acculturation in Canada and the Scandinavian traditions in which she had been raised. These books include **Settlement Poems, One-Eyed Moon Maps, Wake-Pick Poems**, and **The Night Workers of Ragnarok**. **Carnival of Longing** (Turnstone, 1989), a prose/poem written in five sections, deals with the inadequacies of language to communicate the intense desire, loneliness and uncertainty felt during the absence of a lover.

The works of fiction that followed her books of poetry explore the state of mind that comes from the kind of sensory deprivation experienced by people who live in the harsh and unyielding environment of the Arctic or the prairies. **The Prowler** (Red Deer College 1989), a story that spans 2 continents and 4 decades, combines elements of the psychological thriller with the political history of a people trapped by landscape and politics. It won the McNally Robinson Prize in Manitoba and was short listed for the *Books in Canada* first Novel Award and the Alberta Publishers' Association Book Award.

The Substance of Forgetting (Red Deer College, 1992), written in the year of Canada's constitutional referendum, tells the story of a romance between a French-speaking Montreal man and an English-speaking Okanagan Valley woman whose relationship is complicated by language, culture and geography. Her other novels are **The Axe's Edge** (Porcepic, 1983) and **The Guest House** (Porcepic, 1992).

Kristjana Gunnars only work of non-fiction, **Zero Hour** (Red Deer College, 1991) was nominated for the Governor General's Award. This quietly meditative book recounts the author's struggle to come to terms with her father's death from cancer.

Kristjana Gunnars is an associate professor of Creative Writing and Literature at the University of Alberta.

Festival 11 (1993)

VIKING ROLLS

Hardanger bread
8 oz **cream cheese**
1 oz **caviar**

- Moisten Hardanger bread by running cold water over it; wrap in damp cloth and leave for 1/2 hour.
- Spread cream cheese over surface.
- Spread caviar over cream cheese.
- Cut into quarters and roll up.
- GREAT WITH SCHNAPPS

SALMON AND SPINACH ROLLS

fresh spinach
smoked salmon, thinly sliced

- Spread out each slice of salmon on cutting board.
- Cover salmon with a layer of spinach.
- Roll up and slice into 1 inch thick rounds.
- Refrigerate for 2 hours.

SAUCE:

8 oz **sour cream**
1 tsp **mild Swedish mustard**
2 **tomatoes,** diced

- Blend sauce ingredients in blender.
- Pour into fancy flat dish.
- Arrange salmon rolls in sauce according to inclination.
- Decorate with bay leaves.
- ALSO GREAT WITH SCHNAPPS

CHRISTIE HARRIS

A British Columbian since 1908, Christie Harris has been selling children's stories, often internationally, since the 1920s, when she was a primary teacher. Married in 1932, she combined raising five children with an active career as a radio scriptwriter and broadcaster for the CBC.

In 1957 she turned a radio adventure serial into her first book. A few years later, when her husband's work took the family to Prince Rupert, she agreed to do a series of school broadcast scripts on North West Coast Indian cultures, and she became fascinated by the mythology and art. She dropped radio work in the early '60s and began writing a book a year for children and young adults.

Of all her books, she is best known for her 1966 **Raven's Cry**, which Haida artist Bill Reid, who illustrated it, described as "one of the strongest voices speaking for the people of Haida Gwai and their neighbours." A three generation saga, this book has generally been reviewed as a novel, but, according to the author, "It never occured to me that it was a novel. I was just telling the story of the people who produced Charles Edenshaw, telling the story of a line of chiefs who were also artists." **Raven's Cry** was named 1967 Children's Book of the Year by the Canadian Library Association. In 1993 it was republished by Douglas and McIntyre, for adults.

In her more than 60 years of writing, Christie Harris's themes and topics have been dictated by what was going on around her, but again and again the themes of native mythology are to be found in her work. Her awards include a second Canadian Library Association Award for Book of the Year for Children in 1977, the Pacific North West Booksellers' Award, the Vicky Metcalf Award, the International Book of the Year Award and the Canada Council Children's Literature Prize.

In 1980 Christie Harris became a member of the Order of Canada.

This year Orca will publish her 21st book: **Somebody Is Doing Something Weird**.

Festival 6 (1988)

CREATIVE BLOBS

They asked me for a recipe. Me! But how could they know about a kitchen career honed in an inconvenient old house where five kids, mud, wet clotheslines, a doormat dog and an endless stream of CBC-Radio deadlines kept me from even the thought of gourmet cooking?

Last week a grandchild settled beside me and said, "Tell me about the birthday cake that went on fire!" It was her father, briefly in a boarding school, who once thanked me for a *nourishing* tuck box with the news that the guys really liked my "creative blobs". It was his big brother who dubbed Harris cakes as "convertibles" because they so often had to be sauced and served as a pudding. Yet I don't regret one of them. Every domestic disaster ended up in a humour script for CBC's old *Miscellany* program, only to resurface later in some family scene in one of my junior novels. They were as reliable a source of income as my mother's cows and chickens had been. But she, fresh out of Ireland and with five children, much worse equipment and the demands of a farm, turned out treasured memories for *her* kids.

There was THE CHAMP we so often had for lunch: potatoes, mashed, whipped with butter and milk, greened with peas, parsley or chopped green onions and shaped into a well on each plate—a well with a blob of butter melting into a dip for each forkful. Yummmmmy! Then there were the pancakes that I *know* could be peeled off in layers. Yet, even though Susan Musgrave tried to help out by sending a recipe for *Irish pancakes* FROM IRELAND, I still have not found the recipe.

So the best I can do in answer to the Sechelt request is to send what might be classified as a *cautionary tale* for BIRTHDAY CAKE ICING. Try it only if you can use a domestic disaster for entertainment purposes. Okay?

A daughter demanded 7 minute icing for her cake. She was going to DIE if she couln't have 7 minute icing like the rest of the girls. So I tried. The actual cake turned out fine. It was even level after a few judicious cuts with a sharp knife. So I tackled the icing. I hand whipped the egg whites, boiled the sugar syrup until it spun a thread and went at the mixture with my old hand-powered egg beater. But IT had ME beaten. It would not stiffen. So... So I'm the creative type. "Gelatin!" Gelatin would stiffen anything. It actually WORKED! So I quickly slathered the cake with 7 minute icing until it shone like the peaks of the Rocky Mountains. I stuck in the candles before it could change its mind. And when she came home, the birthday girl nearly swooned with delight (and surprise). When the time came, she blew out the candles and picked up the big silver knife. To CUT the cake. Only. . .as the knife went down, down, down, the icing went down, down, down with it. So she pulled the knife up . . .up, up, up and the icing came up, up, up with it. Like elastic. Her sister slashed across the gummy strand with *her* knife and proved that this elastic had two-way-stretch. So all the girls got into the act. I grabbed the cake. Rushed it to the kitchen. And somehow I hacked it into blobs which I put on small plates with a little ice cream. The birthday girl had to make do with—what else?—CREATIVE BLOBS for her birthday.

BETH HILL

Ontario-born Beth Hill served as a regional librarian on the Alaska Highway and later took a position at the Vancouver Public Library. Then about 30 years ago Beth and her husband abandoned the city for rural life on Salt Spring Island. Their island life has been interrupted by a year in North Ireland and another year in England where Beth achieved the Certificate in Pre-historic Archaeology at Cambridge University.

Returning to Salt Spring, she began the research which led to **Indian Petroglyphs of the Pacific Northwest** (Hancock House, 1974) and a later booklet, **Guide to Indian Rock Carvings**. She spent the next two years researching the life of the first woman to circumnavigate the earth in a 19th century sailing ship; the book that resulted was **The Remarkable World of Frances Barkley** (Gray's, 1978).

Upcoast Summers (Horsdal & Schubart), released in 1985, is an edited version of the sea journals of Francis Barrow and his wife Amy, who cruised the Inside Coast of British Columbia in the 1930s. The Barrows were among the first people to record Indian rock art on this coast. Forty years after the Barrows' *Toketie* sailed these waters, the Hills followed in her wake in the *Liza Jane* to fully interpret the Barrows' notes and log entries.

In April 1987 Horsdal & Schubart published Beth Hill's **Sappers: The Royal Engineers in British Columbia**, the first full account of the accomplishments of this distinguished force. Commanded by Colonel Richard Moody, they were sent out from England in 1858 to survey and build the first trails and roads between New Westminster, Hope, Princeton, Yale, Lillooet, Cache Creek and Barkerville, laying the groundwork for the highways that follow these routes today. They also surveyed and planned the townsites of New Westminster, Yale and Princeton and parts of Vancouver.

Exploring the Kettle Valley Railway (Polestar, 1992) brings to life the now-abandoned rail line, the stories of dangerous deeds, massive snow slides, runaway trains, raging forest fires and amazing engineering feats. It gained #3 position on *B.C. Book World's* Best Seller List.

Beth Hill has also written articles for *Westworld, Pacific Yachting, Raincoast Chronicles, Alaska Journal* and *The Islander*. In the spring of 1994, Horsdal & Schubart published **Seven Knot Summers**, which describes visits to coastal people, places and ghosts. H & S also plan to issue a new edition of **The Remarkable World of Frances Barkley**.
Festival 5 (1987)

BLIND CHANNEL CRAB

(from **Seven Knot Summers**, a work in progress)

When we stopped at the Blind Channel store in 1968, we lingered to listen to the elderly woman behind the counter, who was eager to find a buyer for the business. We didn't buy it, but we went away with her recipe for cooking crab.

After you've hauled up your trap and thrown back the undersized crabs, boil (20 minutes) and clean your catch. She told us to make a cream sauce with green peppers, mushrooms and green onions. In a casserole (with lid), pour the cream sauce over the crabmeat and bake in a moderately hot oven for 5 minutes. Then open the casserole, add some wine and a sprinkle of fresh thyme, bake (covered) five minutes longer. "Remove the lid at the table and you'll swoon with the beauty of the fragrance," she said.

Remembering her words, her half-closed eyes and the way she pursed her lips, I find myself drawing in a long breath, recalling those moments on the *Liza Jane* when we plucked off the casserole lid and breathed the ambrosial scent of Blind Channel Crab.

DON HUNTER

"I'm an immigrant Canadian, a writer/story teller, who makes a good living writing in Canada about Canadians," says Don Hunter. A former British Army paratrooper and teacher, he sold his first story to the *Star Weekly* in 1965. He was hired by the Vancouver *Province* in 1969 as a reporter, doing theatre reviews and colour features on the side. Eventually he became a stringer for the *National Enquirer*, several British newspapers, and a regular contributor to the *Star Weekly*.

While working at the *Province's* night news desk and "doing the morning half of raising two daughters", Don Hunter started writing an account of a partial-year's teaching in Fort Nelson, B.C. After eight years of rejections he finally sold the story to CBC where TV producer Jim Swan scripted it. It sat on CBC's shelf for another five years until it was made into the movie **9B**. Don Hunter wrote most of the scripts for the television series that followed.

Sasquatch, Don Hunter's first book, co-authored by Rene Dahinden was published by McClelland & Stewart in 1973 and in paperback by Signet in 1975. McClelland &

Stewart published a revised edition in May 1993.

Many of the tales in Don Hunter's **Spinner's Inlet** (Horsdal & Schubart, 1989), a collection of warm and witty short-short stories set in a fictional community on the Gulf Islands, first appeared in the *Province* newspaper. In a review in The Vancouver's *Sun*, William Rayner described **Spinner's Inlet** as hilarious and poignant in turns, and he recognized in the book's author "an accomplished story-teller with the wit, brevity and keen eye of a good reporter"; the Victoria *Times-Colonist* noted that he portrayed his islanders "with humour, affection and an unerring sense of those qualities that make for effective characters." **Spinner's Inlet** spent eight weeks on the fiction best-seller list in British Columbia and made the short list for the 1990 Stephen Leacock Award for Humour.

Don Hunter writes a general interest column for the Vancouver *Province*.
Festival 7 (1989)

MARY HUNTER'S TATIE POT

Mary was my mother. She was the best, and so was her tatie pot, a traditional dish of the farthest north-west English county of Cumbria, where "Ah's gahn yam" tells you that the first person singular is headed home, and "git thee sel' away yam" suggests you should do the same. On a wet and windblown winter Saturday afternoon, there was no finer or tastier dish to gah yam to.

Several lamb shoulder (or loin if you like) chops (four—six would do)
oil
6 - 8 **medium taties** (Yes, yes - the posh people call them spuds), peeled and quartered
3 - 4 **carrots,** scraped and sliced
1 **small turnip,** peeled and chopped
2 - 3 **good fat onions,** sliced
1 **black pudding (blood sausage) ring**. If you or your doctor do not care for the sound of this, then don't make a tatie pot. It is required.
2 cups **chicken or beef boullion**
Salt, pepper, and Worcestershire sauce, as you prefer.

- Heat your oven to 350°F degrees.
- Brown the chops in a frying pan in some oil.
- Arrange the chops in an oven baking/roasting dish.
- Drape the sliced onions (you can not have too many) on the chops and add the carrots, spuds and turnips.
- Pour on the boullion mixed with Worcestership sauce.
- Add salt and pepper, and add enough water to just cover everything.
- Then—slice the black pudding ring into inch and a half thick rounds and plop these on top of everything.
- Bake at 350°F for about two hours, or until everything under the surface is tender and the top of the black pudding slices are crisp and almost crunchy.
- If it needs thickening, use a standard cornstarch or flour and water mix, or just mash the spuds and turnip up in the gravy.
- Spoon it up onto plates/dishes.
- Have thick wedges of fresh bread and a plate of soft butter ready at the side.
- And some wine.

DOROTHY THOMAS'S WELSH CAKES

Dorothy Thomas was my mother-in-law, a petite and proper Welsh woman who on Saturday afternoons filled her immaculate home in Cardiff with the warm and special smells of these griddle delights.

8 oz **flour**
5 oz **butter**
3 oz **sugar**
3 oz **currants/raisins**
1/4 tsp **allspice**

1/2 tsp **baking powder**
1 **egg**
pinch salt
1 tbsp **light cream**

- Sift flour, baking powder and salt, rub in butter.
- Add other dry ingredients.
- Beat egg lightly and combine with cream.
- Add enough of this mix to the dry ingredients to make a stiff dough.
- Roll out on a floured board to 1/2 inch thickness.
- Cut into rounds and cook on a greased griddle three to four minutes each side or until golden brown.
- Cool, sprinkle with sugar, serve with butter and raspberry jam.

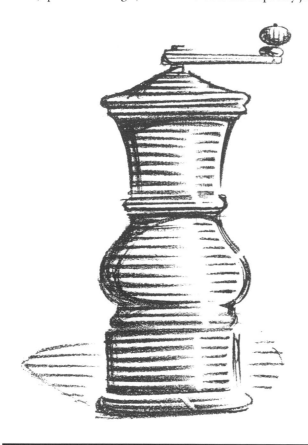

EILEEN KERNAGHAN

Eileen Kernaghan, co-owner of a bookstore in Burnaby, is the author of a pre-history fantasy trilogy: **Journey to Aprilioth** (Ace, 1980) which won a PORGY Award (Original Paper-back Fantasy) from the *West Coast Review of Books*; **Songs from the Drowned Lands** (Ace, 1983) which won the Canadian Science Fiction and Fantasy Award; and **The Sarsen Witch** (Ace, 1989). Although she confesses that her experience as an ax warrior is minimal, her stories are true to what is historically documented about Bronze Age Britain. "I write about what could have taken place."

"Nobody really chooses to be a fantasy writer," Eileen Kernaghan says, "and I can't imagine how you would train for a career as a fantasist." Her own background includes an isolated rural background and an insatiable appetite for books—fairy tales, ghost stories, Greek myths, old pulp magazines, and tales of romance and high adventure in exotic lands.

Eileen Kernaghan's short science fiction and fantasy has appeared in *Galaxy, Space and Time, Womanspace, Tesseracts, Room of One's Own, On Spec*, and **The Window of Dreams** (an anthology of Canadian children's literature, Methuen, 1986), **The Blue Jean Collection** (Thistledown, 1992) and **Ark of Ice** (Pottersfield, 1992). Her poetry has been published in *Prism International, Room of One's Own, The Magazine of Speculative Poetry* and *Magic Realism*.

Her only non-fiction work is **Walking after Midnight** (Berkely, 1990), on reincarnation and near-death experiences; it was co-authored by film-maker Johnathon Kay.

She also co-authored the handbook **The Upper Left-Hand Corner: A Writer's Guide for the Northwest** with Edith Surridge, Patrick Kernaghan and Ross Westergaard. It includes information on markets, copyright, manuscript preparation and much more.

With science fiction and fantasy writers Mary Choo, Michael Coney, Teresa Plowright and Rhea Rose, she formed the writers group, *The Lonely Cry*, to draw more attention to west coast sf and fantasy writers. Their emblem, a wolf howling at the moon, heads their regular bulletin.

Festival 2 (1984)

EILEEN'S OUT-OF-THIS-WORLD VEGETARIAN CURRY

1 large head cauliflower
1 medium-sized potato
19 oz **can garbanzo beans, with liquid**
1 tbsp **butter or vegetable oil**
1 tsp **ground coriander**
1 tsp **ground cumin**
1 tsp **turmeric**
1/4 tsp **cayenne pepper**, or to taste
1/4 tsp **ground cloves**

1/4 tsp **cinnamon**
1/4 tsp **ground ginger**
3 cloves **garlic,** minced
1/2 **onion,** slivered
salt to taste
2 tbsp **lemon juice**, or to taste
1 **medium-sized tomato,** chopped
2 cups **spinach leaves,** coarsely chopped
  (optional)

- Trim and wash the cauliflower and break it up into small flowerets.
- Scrub the potato and boil it in salted water until it is nearly tender, but not quite done.
- Heat the oil or butter in a saucepan or skillet and stir in the spices, garlic and onion. Saute over medium heat, stirring constantly, for 3 to 4 minutes.
- Stir in the garbanzo beans and liquid, mashing some of the beans with a fork or potato masher to thicken the curry.
- Add the cauliflower, cover the pan and simmer for 5 minutes, stirring often.
- Meanwhile cut the parboiled potato into small cubes.
- Add the potato, stir, cover again, and leave to simmer for 10 minutes.
- Then add the tomato, spinach and lemon juice, and stir, uncovered for another few minutes before serving.
- Serve hot with rice, chutney and other condiments.
- Serves 4 - 6.

WELSH CAKES

3 cups **sifted all-purpose flour**
1 1/2 tsp **baking powder**
1/2 tsp **baking soda**
1 1/4 tsp **salt**
1 cup **white sugar**
1 tsp **nutmeg**

1 cup **shortening**
  (or 1/2 shortening, 1/2 butter)
1 cup **currants**
2 **eggs**
6 tbsp **milk**

- Sift dry ingredients into bowl.
- Cut in shortening.
- Add currants.
- Beat eggs and milk together. Add to fruit-flour mixture, mixing well.
- Divide dough into 3 or 4 parts. Roll out about 1/4 inch thick on lightly floured board.
- Cut into small rounds with cookie cutter.
- Bake on heated griddle, 350°F about 10 to 12 minutes on each side until nicely browned and cooked.
- Makes 3 dozen.

W. P. (BILL) KINSELLA

"I beat my head against the walls of North American literature for 20 years to become an overnight sensation," writes Edmonton-born W.P. Kinsella. Now famous for his novels of Indians and baseball players (though he is quick to point out that he is neither), Bill Kinsella underwent a long apprenticeship as a short story writer but by 1968, when he graduated from the Iowa Writers' Workshop, he had 61 stories in print. **Dance Me Outside** (Oberon Press, 1977), his first short story collection, featured a native narrator named Silas Ermineskin recounting the adventures of a band of fictional Indians on the Hobbema Reserve, a non-fictional reserve in Alberta. Asked how Indians felt about his stories, Bill Kinsella said "I write about people who just happen to be Indians." He describes finding the Ermineskin "voice" as "like finding a vein of gold," and he continued in this vein with his later story collections, **The Fencepost Chronicles** (1986) which won the 1987 Stephen Leacock Award, **Red Wolf, Red Wolf** (1987), and **The Miss Hobbema Pageant**, (1989).

But Bill Kinsella had stumbled on a second vein of gold with the baseball stories that he included in collections like **The Thrill of the Grass** (1984), **The Further Adventures of Slugger McBatt** (1988),

The Dixon Cornbelt League and Other Baseball Stories (1993).

However, it was his 1982 novel **Shoeless Joe,** a mystical baseball fantasy, that captured both readers' and critics' attention. **Shoeless Joe** made him the first non-American to win the prestigious Houghton Mifflin Literary Fellowship; it garnered 5 other awards, and was made into the hit movie **Field of Dreams** (Twentieth Century Fox), starring Kevin Costner. Bill Kinsella's other novels include **The Iowa Baseball Confederacy** (1990) and **Box Socials** (1991).

Two Spirits Soar celebrates the distinctive talent of Cree artist Allen Sapp, who specializes in paintings depicting native life as he remembers it on the Red Pheasant Reserve near North Battleford, as well as his friendship with his mentor, Dr. Allan Gonor. Festival 6 (1988)

BOLOGNA SOUP

8 ounces **tomato juice**
1/8 tsp **baking soda**
8 ounces **whole milk**

3 slices **bologna**
black pepper
parsley, basil (optional)

- Place tomato juice in a saucepan, heat, adding baking soda.
- Stir.
- Add milk.
- Dice bologna and add to mixture.
- No need to cook, simply heat and season to taste with black pepper.
- Parsley or basil may be added if desired.

PEPPERS TRIESTE

This is modified from a recipe of my Yugoslavian grandmother, Baba Drobney.

2 **large green bell peppers**
ground beef (enough to fill pepper halves)
salt, pepper

A-1 steak sauce
mild yellow cheese

- Halve green peppers vertically and clean.
- Take sufficient ground beef to fill pepper halves, and lace it liberally with pepper, salt and A-1 Steak Sauce.
- Microwave the ground beef until about 3/4 cooked through.
- Microwave pepper halves until slightly soft.
- Stuff pepper halves with meat mixture.
- Microwave until beef is cooked—about 3 minutes.
- Place a large slice of mild yellow cheese on each pepper half.
- Microwave until cheese is melted.

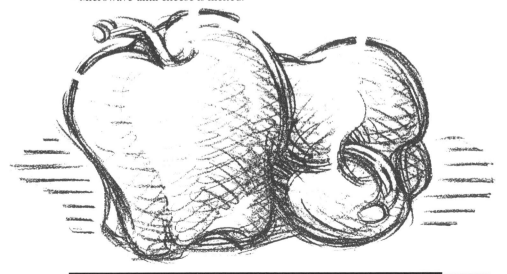

ROBERT KROETSCH

Born and raised in Alberta, Robert Kroetsch graduated from the University of Alberta, then spent the next 6 years working on river boats on the MacKenzie River and working for the USAF in Labrador before enrolling in graduate school in the United States. From 1958 to 1978 he taught English at the State University of New York at Binghamton where he was co-editor of the literary journal *Boundary 2*. He returned to Canada in 1978 to join the Faculty of English at the University of Manitoba as Distinguished Professor of Canadian Literature; in 1993 he retired to Victoria, British Columbia.

Robert Kroetsch won international success first as a novelist, then as a poet and most recently as an essayist. His novels include **But We Are Exiles** (1977); **The Words Of My Roaring; The Studhorse Man** (1969/1982) which earned him the Governor General's Award for Fiction; **Badlands** (1981); **What The Crow Said** (1983); **Gone Indian** (1971); and **Alibi** (1984). His latest novel, **The Puppeteer**, published by Random House in 1992, a "sort of murder mystery" (although no murder actually occurs), has been described by Douglas Glover in *Books in Canada* as "a

critique of conventional theories of meaning and the traditional novel".

Although he had been writing poetry in his mid-thirties, his first poetry collection, **Stone Hammer Poems** did not appear until 1976, but it marked the beginning of his strong influence on future Canadian poetry. **The Sad Phoenician** was published shortly after his return to Canada. **Seed Catalogue** (1977) received wide acclaim; the *Globe and Mail's* reviewer wrote: "No other book of recent poetry, and few in fiction, sets out with more wit and precision the connections of place and poetry. He is an experimental writer of the first rank." **Excerpts From The Real World** followed in 1986. **Completed Field Notes** (1989), a collection of his long poems, was published in 1989, bringing an end to the series of poetry books begun with **Seed Catalogue** where the dominant images are agricultural or natural.

Seventeen of his critical essays are collected in **The Lovely Treachery Of Words** (1989).

Festival 8 (1990) & Workshops Summer 1991 and Summer 1993

AVGOLEMONO SOUP
(Egg and Lemon Soup)

5 1/2 cups **chicken broth**
1/2 tsp **salt**
1/2 tsp **white pepper**
1/2 cup **white rice**

3 **eggs**
juice of two lemons
1 tbsp **cold water**

- Bring the chicken broth to a boil. Season it with the salt and pepper.
- Add the rice, and cook over low to moderate heat until rice is fluffy and done. Remove from the heat.
- In a large bowl beat the eggs until light and frothy.
- Add the lemon juice and one tablespoon of cold water, and stir until mixed.
- Slowly blend half of the liquid of the soup into the egg and lemon mixture while stirring it constantly.
- Pour this mixture slowly into the rice and remaining liquid.
- Stir until well mixed.
- Serve at once.
- Serves four to five.

(As prepared by Robert Kroetsch's wife, Smaro Kamboureli)

TYROPITTA
(Phyllo feta pie)

1 box **Krinos pastry phyllo leaves** (available in most supermarkets in the frozen foods section).
1 1/2 lbs **feta cheese** (not too soft)
dash nutmeg
7 **eggs** (at room temperature)
2 tbsp **cold water**
1 cup **unsalted butter,** melted
1 cup **parsley,** chopped
200 grams **mozzarella,** shredded

For the sauce:
1/2 cup **unsalted butter**
5-7 tbsp **flour**
1 cup **milk** (at room temperature)

- Preheat oven to 375˚F.
- Thaw the phyllo leaves (it takes two to three hours).
- In a small saucepan make the sauce by melting 1/2 cup of unsalted butter until frothy over moderate heat. Then slowly add the flour while stirring constantly. Remove from heat, add the milk while stirring. When well blended and smooth, remove from heat and cool.

(Continued on pg. 72)

- Unfold the phyllo leaves, spread them flat, and keep them covered with a moistened tea towel to prevent them from drying out.
- Cut the feta cheese in small chunks, and crumble in a food processor.
- Place in a large bowl. Add the parsley, six eggs, mozzarella, nutmeg, and the sauce. Blend well.
- Using a brush, butter well all sides of a pan. Spread six phyllo leaves, brushing the first five leaves with the melted butter.
- Spread the feta filling evenly on the top leaf.
- Cover it with several layers of phyllo, brushing each one with the remaining melted butter.
- With scissors trim the edges of the phyllo.
- With a sharp knife cut the pie diagonally from both sides while taking care not to cut all the way to the bottom layer.
- Put in preheated oven. After three minutes, open the oven and sprinkle the pie with water. Close the oven.
- Mix the remaining egg and two tablespoons of water. Open the oven again and brush the mixture on the pie.
- Reduce heat to 350°F. Bake for twenty minutes to half an hour, or until crust is golden brown.

(As prepared by Robert Kroetsch's wife, Smaro Kamboureli)

PATRICK *L* ANE

Patrick Lane, who was born in Nelson, B.C., left high school to work as an unskilled labourer in construction, sawmilling and logging, later becoming an industrial first-aid-man in sawmills because it paid an extra fifteen cents an hour; he has also been a salesman, an office manager, and a corporate industrial accountant. But writing with serious intent began for him as early as 1958 when he was just nineteen, and as a result, he has spent much of his life wandering three continents as an itinerant poet.

During the 1960s Patrick Lane collaborated with bill bissett and Seymour Mayne in the establishment of the little press, Very Stone House, which was responsible for producing a number of important poetry collections, among them Lane's **Letters from the Savage Mind** (1966). He ran Very Stone House from Vancouver until 1970 when his life resumed its transient course; the press was then renamed Very Stone House in Transit and issued its publications from various spots across Canada for the next ten years.

Patrick Lane has published thirteen volumes of poetry. His **Poems, New & Selected** (Oxford University Press) won the Governor General's award in 1979; **Selected Poems** (Oxford) won the Canadian Authors Association Award for Poetry in 1988. Among his most recent books are the poetry collection **Winter** (Coteau Books), nominated for the Governor General's Award in 1991, and a collection of poems for children titled **Milford and Me** (Coteau). **Mortal Remains**, his newest poetry collection, published in 1992 by Exile Editions, was also nominated for the highest Canadian literary award and has received excellent reviews.

His short stories, published in periodicals such as *The Tamarack Review, Malahat Review, Canadian Literature, The Chicago Review* and *The Times Literary Supplement*, have received many awards and have been included in **Best American Stories** and **Best Canadian Stories**. A collection of his short fiction, **How Do You Spell Beautiful,** was published by Fifth House in 1992.

Patrick Lane has served as writer-in-residence at the Universities of Manitoba, Concordia, Alberta and Toronto, and he has taught creative writing and Canadian Literature at the Universities of Saskatchewan and Victoria.

Festival 10 (1992) & Workshops Summer 1988, Fall 1992 and Fall 1993

CHICKEN A LA PATRICK

Herewith my recipe for the best quick chicken dish ever created!

4 **half breasts of chicken** (range birds if possible)
juice of 6 lemons
flour
2 oz **good scotch whiskey**

- Take two double chicken breasts, separate from bone, and pound until flat.
- Take the juice of six lemons and drench the chicken, allowing it to marinate for two hours (turn chicken regularly).
- After marinating, dredge lightly in flour and fry to a golden brown.
- Serve hot, drenching with two ounces of good scotch whiskey and flambe. Serve immediately.
- Serves four.

Note: This recipe can be doubled or tripled only be careful of the scotch— you don't want an explosion!

JOHN LAZARUS

A uthor of more than a dozen highly successful stage plays, John Lazarus is one of Canada's foremost playwrights. His play **Babel Rap** (first produced in 1972) is one of the most frequently produced plays written in Canada, and when revived in 1990, played to sold-out audiences at Toronto's Canadian Stage Theatre and received rave reviews. **Dreaming and Duelling** is a collaboration first produced in 1980.

His other plays include **The Late Blumer, Village of Idiots, Genuine Fakes, David for Queen**, and the 1990 Touchstone Theatre (Vancouver) and Belfry Theatre (Victoria) hit, **Homework & Curtains**. *Homework for Men*, the first act of **Homework & Curtains**, was chosen to open the annual New Play Festival in London, England, in May 1992. **Homework & Curtains** has been published in paperback by Playwrights Press, Toronto. His one-man play **Medea's Disgust** was performed at the 1991 Vancouver Fringe Festival; a radio version was produced on CBC's Stereo Drama.

His "saga" of four children's plays written for Vancouver's Green Thumb Theatre for Young People— **Schoolyard Games, Not So Dumb, Night Light**, and **Secrets**—was published as **Not So Dumb: Four Plays for Young People** by Coach House Press in 1993. These unsentimental studies of the pains and pressures children endure on the road to maturity have enjoyed over 30 productions in Canada, the U.S., Great Britain and New Zealand.

John Lazarus also writes for radio and television and occasionally acts. He was story editor for the Atlantis/CBC-TV program *Mom P.I.*

His stage adaptation of Hans Christian Andersen's **The Nightingale** opened in Toronto in February 1994; a radio version for CBC is currently in the works. Recently he has been writing **The Trials of Eddy Haymour** for the Western Canada Theatre Company of Kamloops, **Straight Guys in Love** for Vancouver's Arts Club Theatre, and **Kiddie Theatre Hell** on a Canada Council "A" Grant.

Workshops Spring 1991 and Summer 1992

MULTICULTURED YOGURT

500 gm **plain yogurt**
2 **bananas**
3 tbsp **crystallized ginger**

3 tbsp **real maple syrup**
powdered cinnamon - to taste

* Slice bananas.
* Chop ginger very fine.
* Blend bananas & ginger into yogurt.
* Blend in maple syrup.
* Add a dash of cinnamon.
* Serve garnished with cinnamon sticks.
* Serves 2.

BREAKFAST EGGS FOR TWO

4 **eggs**
1/2 cup **cheddar cheese (extra-strong)**
1 **small onion** (or 1/2 medium onion)

1 tbsp **oregano**
salt and pepper to taste

* Dice onion and saute in an oiled skillet. When the onion begins to turn soft and transparent, break in eggs.
* Grate cheese onto the eggs.
* As eggs begin to turn opaque, begin scrambling them.
* Add oregano, salt and pepper, scrambling as you go.
* Serve on whole wheat toast.
* Serve freshly squeezed grapefruit juice and coffee on the side.
* For variations, add a dash of Tabasco or Worcestershire, OR a teaspoon of caviar (but preferably not all three).

CHARLES LYNCH

C harles Lynch began his newspaper career in St. John, New Brunswick, in 1936 and spent more than 50 years as a reporter, war correspondent, columnist and commentator on international and political affairs. In time he also became very familiar to radio listeners and television viewers.

In 1976 he was elected president of the Parliamentary Press Gallery and awarded an honorary doctorate of laws by Mount Allison University. He became an Officer of the Order of Canada in 1977, and was named to the Canadian News Hall of Fame in 1981.

An incomparably witty story-teller both in person and in print, Charles Lynch looks at politics and politicians with humour and generosity. He is the author of **You Can't Print That** (1983), **Race For The Rose** (1984) and **A Funny Way To Run A Country** (1986). In **The Lynch Mob** (1988) he rates Canada's postwar prime ministers in terms of their effectiveness, then tells anecdotes to prove it; having covered all nine of them in his journalistic career, he knows their strengths and shortcomings better than most! In 1991 he turned from politics to his favourite pastime—fishing—in **Fishing with Simon** (1991), the Simon of the title being his long-time fishing companion, Simon Reisman, negotiator of the Free Trade Agreement.

Although for many years his career and main hobby was prime minister-watching, Charles Lynch bicycles, sails, plays billiards and fishes, for all of which he has won awards. (He has also appeared as a circus clown, harmonica soloist with various orchestras, and danced twice with the National Ballet!) He is the honorary president of the Rouen Butchers' Association; he was a competitor in the Great Centennial Balloon Race in 1979, and is the co-holder of the North American speed rcord for passenger trains, 140 miles an hour.

Festival 7 (1989)

CHARLES LYNCH'S 15-MINUTE
NEW BRUNSWICK STYLE BAKED BEANS

One regular can **baked beans in molasses** per person
Two strips of **breakfast bacon** per person, cut into bits
One **clove of garlic** per person
Two dashes of **Worcestershire sauce** per person
One teaspoon of **mild mustard** per person
Two good dollops of **Crosby's Barbados molasses** per person

- Into large fry pan on high heat, place bacon bits. When they start sizzling, stir until fat flies. Turn heat down to medium and empty in the cans of beans. Stir.
- Add molasses. Stir.
- Crush garlic into the pan, including garlic husks.
- Add Worcestershire sauce. Stir.
- Add mild mustard. Stir.
- Let mixture bubble for five minutes, stir and taste.
- Sprinkle with salt and pepper from grinder.
- The beans should be ready to eat in 15 minutes, but will not suffer if left on simmer for another half hour. If wait will be longer than that, turn off and reheat when needed. In the unlikely event of any beans left over, they make great sandwiches, cold.

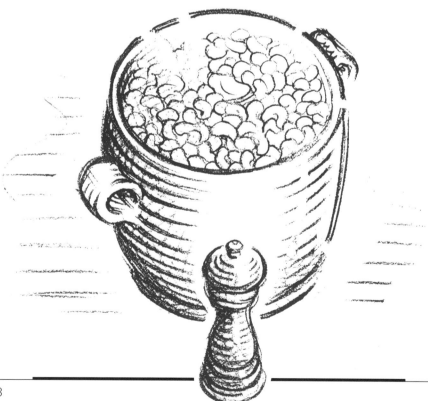

McCALL & CLARKSON

Christina McCall is an editor, political commentator and author who has worked for *Maclean's, Saturday Night* and *The Globe & Mail*. Her work, praised by Robert Fulford for its 'brilliant social insights and superb prose', has won her a dozen national awards, including the President's Medal of the University of Western Ontario, a Southam Fellowship at the University of Toronto, and a National Magazine Award gold medal. Her book, **Grits: An Intimate Portrait of the Liberal Party**, was described by *The Globe & Mail* as "no less than an anatomy of political power in Canada which should be read by everyone who wants to know who really runs this country." Short-listed for the Governor General's Award, it won the Canadian Authors' Association Book of the Year Award and was the No. 1 non-fiction bestseller for twenty-two weeks.

Her partner, Stephen Clarkson is a social activist, having run for mayor of Toronto, served on the editorial board of the Canadian Forum, and been president of the University League for Social Reform for many years. He teaches politics at the University of Toronto, where he specializes in the political economy of the Canadian-American relationship; comments regularly on the French and English media; and has published several books in Canada and abroad. His **Canada and the Reagan Challenge** won the John Porter Prize in the Social Sciences.

McCall and Clarkson are co-authors of a major study of the Trudeau era, **Trudeau and Our Times** (McClelland and Stewart). Volume 1, subtitled **The Magnificent Obsession**, published in 1990, was a major best seller in French and English and won the Governor General's Award with the citation, "In prose that is lucid and gripping...the authors have brought the public and private selves of Pierre Trudeau together, illuminating in the process his overwhelming impact on the country's political life." Volume 2, subtitled **The Fateful Delusion**, is scheduled to be published in 1994.

Festival 9 (1991)

CHICKEN PILAF A LA GOUGEON

This is comfort food at our place, a staple recipe Christina acquired
when she was a public affairs commentator on a CBC-Ottawa daytime TV
show in the Sixties, and the great Canadian cook and food editor, Helen
Gougeon, travelled from Montreal once a week to talk about food on the
program. Our three daughters have loved it since childhood and we make
it, now that they are all in the twenties, when they come home from their
various graduate schools or jobs needing comfort or counselling. It's good
with leftover roast chicken from a Sunday dinner, but best of all made from
chicken breasts poached for the purpose. In summer, we leave out the
almonds and sprinkle chopped coriander from our garden over each
portion as a garnish but that changes the taste, making it more California-
here-we-come than Canada-here-we-are on an autumn night.

2-3 tbsp **butter**
2 cups **cooked chicken,** cut into strips
1/2 cup **onions,** diced
1/2 tsp **each oregano and thyme or other fresh/dried herb of choice**
salt, pepper to taste
1 cup **uncooked converted rice**
2-1/2 cups **chicken stock**
1/2 cup **chopped fresh or canned tomatoes,** drained
1/2 cup sliced **almonds**
parsley, chopped

- Melt butter in a large saucepan. (If you're watching fat intake carefully,
  you can substitute two or three tablespoons of chicken broth for the
  butter).
- Add onion and cook until soft.
- Add chicken, herbs, salt and pepper.
- Add rice and cook, stirring occasionally, for 5 minutes on low heat.
- Slowly add chicken stock.
- Add tomatoes and nuts, bring to a boil and cover and simmer for 20
  minutes or until rice is tender.
- Do not stir.
- Sprinkle parsley on top of each serving.
- Serves six picky eaters or 4 hungry ones.

RED PEPPER SAUCE FOR PASTA

We make a big batch of this sauce for the freezer in early September when full bushels of gorgeous, locally grown red peppers are sold at vegetable markets in Southern Ontario at a price you pay for a mere three or four in supermarkets the rest of the year. On a winter week night, when we're too busy for elaborate cookery, a quart of the sauce gently reheated makes the kitchen smell like a late summer afternoon and the pasta it's served over taste like Tuscany. The sauce is also good spooned over a slice of frittata or mashed into a baked potato.

4 **red peppers** (approximately 1 lb)
2 **onions** (about 1 lb)
1/4 cup **olive oil**
1 tbsp **garlic,** finely chopped

1/2 tsp **dried, hot red pepper flakes**
2 cups **chicken broth** (preferably homemade)
salt and freshly ground pepper to taste
1/4 cup **fresh basil,** finely chopped

- Cut peppers in half. Cut out and discard core, veins and seeds, and chop coarsely. (Yield should be about four cups.)
- Peel and coarsely chop enough onions to yield about four cups.
- Heat the oil in a deep skillet and add the peppers. Cook, stirring, about five minutes.
- Add onions, garlic and red pepper flakes and cook, stirring often, about two minutes.
- Add broth, salt and pepper.
- Cover and cook 15 minutes.
- Pour mixture into the container of a food processor or blender and blend thoroughly.
- Pour the mixture into a saucepan and bring to the boil. Let cook about two minutes.
- Stir in fresh basil.
- Serve over pasta, with grated parmesan cheese on the side.
- If fresh basil isn't available, a small amount of chopped parsley sprinkled over each portion enhances the look of the dish, but neither herb is really necessary. The onions and peppers meld into a wonderful flavour on their own.
- YIELD: About four cups.

STUART McLEAN

Early in 1991, Toronto-based journalist and CBC radio commentator Stuart McLean travelled to small town Canada in search of the material for a book about this country. He had three criteria in mind when he chose the towns he would visit. "First of all, I was looking for people with interesting stories to tell. Secondly, I wanted to tell the story of Canada, so I was looking for a certain 'Canadianness', for a red thread that would run through all of the towns. Third was the history of the place. I was looking for the kind of things that put you in touch with the past." What he found in those seven small towns became the subject of his book **Welcome Home: Travels in Small Town Canada**, a book one reviewer called "a tonic for our national ills." In 1993 the Canadian Authors Association awarded **Welcome Home** best non-fiction book of the year.

In spite of his affinity for small towns, Stuart McLean has never been a small town boy. Born, raised and educated in Montreal, he received his B.A. from Sir George Williams University. After a few years in the Student Affairs Department at Dawson College in Montreal, he began writing for local CBC television and radio programs. In 1976 he became an Associate Producer at *Morningside*; five years later he became Executive Producer of *Sunday Morning*, CBC Radio's flagship current affairs programme. Since 1984, he has been the director of Broadcast Journalism at the Ryerson Polytechnic University.

Stuart McLean told stories on *Morningside* every Monday morning from 1985 to 1993, his subjects ranging from wooden pencils to alligator pie. He co-wrote, with Kevin Sullivan, the feature-length movie, **Looking for Miracles** and contributed to **The New Morningside Papers**, published in 1987. His first book, **The Morningside World of Stuart McLean**, was published by Viking in 1989.

Winner of an ACTRA Award for his documentary on the Jonestown Massacre in 1979, he has been nominated for 3 other ACTRA awards since then. He has also won a B'nai Brith Human Rights Award for a report on hunger in Canada, and was co-nominated for the Gordon Sinclair Award for Excellence in Broadcast Journalism.

Festival 11 (1993)

CHICKEN FAJITAS

This is a fast, easy, and delicious supper. You'll need:

a couple of chicken breasts
a package of soft tortillas
juice of enough fresh limes for marinade
  (enough to cover the chicken)
fresh garlic
fresh ginger
some tomatoes

some grated cheese
some chopped onion
some red (or green) peppers
an avocado or two
a jar of salsa
sour cream
any other garnish that appeals to you

- Take a couple of skinless de-boned chicken breasts (I favour the pre-skinned, de-boned ones you can buy in bulk from the supermarket—we keep a box in the freezer and dip into it whenever we need a meal in a hurry) and chop them (the breasts) into bite-sized cubes.
- Throw them in a bowl with the lime juice, a bit of crushed garlic and some grated ginger. Leave them to marinate (at least one hour—best is eight hours).
- About 45 minutes before you want to serve supper make guacamole. Scoop out the avocado and mash it up as if you were making mashed potatoes. Add a spoonful or two of the salsa. There. You are finished.
- Put it in a bowl on the table.
- Now grate the cheese and put it in a bowl on the table.
- Now chop up the onions and the tomatoes and put them in two separate bowls on the table.
- If you want to be fancy, cut the red peppers into strips and throw them on the Bar-B-Que until they are cooked. If you don't want to be fancy, fry them up. If you are really in a hurry, serve them raw.
- We are in the home stretch now and your table should be looking pretty festive.
- Heat up the tortillas in the microwave (one at a time—about ten seconds each), then throw them in the oven (set at warm) to keep them hot. If you don't have a microwave, heat them in the oven. They should be soft—like a pancake—not crispy.
- Now dump the chicken and the marinade in a fry pan and cook until the chicken is ready to eat. Put the chicken and the marinade in a bowl on the table. Give everyone a tortilla (or two, or three) and tell them to fill it (them) with whatever they want, roll it up and eat it like a hot dog.

PRETTY GOOD BAR-B-QUE CHICKEN

You'll need:

chicken legs
the juice of enough fresh limes to make marinade
fresh garlic
fresh ginger

The hardest part of this recipe is remembering to begin step one 24 hours before you want to cook the chicken.

Step one:
- Take as many chicken legs as you want to cook and remove the skin. This might be the hardest part of this recipe because if you are like me you'll find that the skin keeps slipping out of your hands when you try to pull it over the knobby end of the drumstick. Also your hands get wet and cold and there is no way around it. The only thing yuckier than a pile of raw chicken skins is the thought of eating them. The last time I skinned chicken I used a piece of paper towel to grip the skin. It doesn't slip as much that way.
- Once you have the skin off you have to perform a little operation on each leg. Cut the two tendons at the knobby end of each drumstick and push the meat up the bone so it forms a sort of lump at the far end (the meaty end). When you are finished each leg should look like a lollypop (sort of).
- Now it's time to marinate the chicken. Squeeze enough lime juice into a bowl to cover the chicken legs and add freshly grated ginger (you decide how much) and as much freshly crushed garlic as you feel comfortable with.
- Put the bowl into the fridge and leave it there for twenty- four hours.
- ***Helpful hint:*** a friend of mine likes to marinate things in a plastic grocery bag rather than a bowl; this way she can move the meat around without having to touch it.

Step two:
- Remove the chicken from the fridge and Bar-B-Que.

FLORENCE McNEIL

Vancouver-born Florence McNeil made her writing name first as a poet, then as a writer of children's fiction and most recently as the author of adult fiction, and she has won critical acclaim and awards in all three careers.

Of her eight books of poetry, the major ones include **Emily** (Clarke, Irwin, 1975), **Ghost Towns** (McClel-land & Stewart, 1975), **A Balancing Act** (M & S, 1979), **The Overlanders** (Thistledown, 1982), and **Barkerville** (Thistledown, 1984), selections from which won a National Magazine Award in 1980. Her most recent book of poems, **Swimming Out of History: New and Selected Poems** (Oolichan, 1992) is a collection culled from 20 years of her work, and includes her long poem "Walhachin" which had been published in book form by Fiddlehead in 1972.

Her first book for children, **Miss P. and Me**, went through four editions: Clarke, Irwin, 1982; Scholastic, 1984; Harper & Row, 1984; Berkely/Pacer, 1986. It was also made into a film by Atlantis for the CBC series *Sons and Daughters*. Her second novel for children, **All Kinds of Magic** (Groundwood, 1984) won an "Our Choice"

Award, and her third, the young adult novel, **Catriona's Island** (Ground-wood, 1988), won the Sheila Egoff Silver Award. She has edited two anthologies of poetry for young people: **Here is a Poem: An Anthology of Canadian Poetry** (League of Canadian Poets, 1984) and **Do the Whales Jump at Night: An Anthology of Canadian Poetry for Children** (Ground-wood, 1990). Her book of ideas for teaching poetry, **When is a Poem**, was published by the League of Canadian Poets in 1980.

Florence McNeil's "play for voices", **Barkerville**, was broadcast on the CBC's Hornby Collection in 1980. A subsequent stage version was workshopped by Vancouver's New Play Centre and produced at North Vancouver's Presentation House.

Her most recent work, **Breathing Each Other's Air**, a novel for adults, was published in Spring 1994.

Florence McNeil is in demand as a teacher of creative writing across Canada and the United States. She is now concentrating on fiction for adults.

Festival 1 (1983) & Workshops Summer 1990

These are two traditional Hebridean Scots recipes. My mum's scones and oatcakes are always the first to go at any gathering.

MY MOTHER'S AUTHENTIC SCOTCH OATCAKES

1 1/2 cups **medium oatmeal** (not rolled oats)
pinch to 1/4 tsp **salt**
1/2 tsp **baking soda**

1 1/2 tbsp **melted shortening**
enough cold water to mix

- Mix oatmeal, soda and salt.
- Add melted shortening and enough cold water to mix (don't use too much water).
- Turn out on well-floured board and press out with hands until 1/3-inch thick.
- Shape into a round and cut in triangles.
- Cook till they seem crisp.
  Note: Can be baked in oven at 350°F for 15 - 20 minutes or on top of stove on griddle at medium heat (turn over when slightly browned).

MY MOTHER'S FAMOUS TRADITIONAL SCOTCH SCONES

2 cups **all-purpose flour,** preferably
  unbleached
2 tsp **baking powder**
1/4 tsp **baking soda**
pinch **salt**

2 heaping tbsp **vegetable shortening**
1 or 2 **eggs,** beaten slightly
1 cup **buttermilk,** mixed with beaten
  eggs

- Sift flour, baking powder, baking soda and salt. Mix in vegetable shortening, add buttermilk and egg mixture.
- Knead slightly on floured board, shape into round ball and press out with the palm of your hand until 1/2-inch thick.
- Cut into four pieces.
- Bake in oven at 425°F to 450°F for 10 or 15 minutes.
  Note: They can also be cooked on top of the stove at medium heat.
- Serve hot or cold.

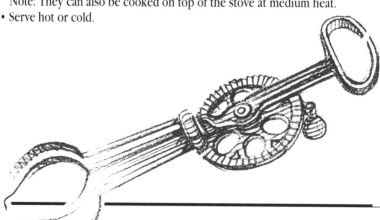

MARY MEIGS

Mary Meigs is one of the eight women who portray themselves in *The Company of Strangers*, the semi-documentary National Film Board production that was released in 1990 to overwhelming critical and popular acclaim. Because she was too busy writing and painting, she hadn't been among the hundreds who answered the NFB's 1988 advertisement inviting "older women" to take part in a film, but director Cynthia Scott and script writer Gloria Demers sought her out and broke down her resistance. The public is the richer as a result, both because of her role in the film and because of the book—**In the Company of Strangers** (Talonbooks, 1991)—that she later wrote, a book that begins with the story of her film experience and unfolds into a gentle, intricate meditation on the experience of time, old age, magic and the bonds of friendship. "We are formed," she says, "by everyone we meet, out of resistance or emulation, but our choice of friends often seems to come from the pressure of whatever in us wants to grow, or refuses to grow."

Born in Philadelphia in 1917, artist and writer Mary Meigs grew up cossetted in wealthy surroundings where she was not allowed to be what she was—a lesbian. Not until she was sixty years old did she finally write openly about her life. Her book, **Lily Briscoe: a Self Portrait** (Talonbooks, 1981) is both an autobiography and a memoir, a portrait of herself, her family and her friends. The book is also about the use we make of ourselves and others. "One gives up power by sharing oneself with others," she says. "In another sense, one gains from receiving from other people...my belief is that sharing of oneself is much less dangerous than one thinks."

Mary Meigs continued to share her past in her next books. **The Medusa Head** (Talonbooks, 1983), is a sensitive psychological study of the stormy three-way lesbian relationship in which she was involved with fiction writers Marie-Claire Blais and "Andree". **The Box Closet** (Talonbooks), which followed in 1987, was based on her parents' diaries and letters which she discovered in an attic closet of the family's Washington, D.C. home after her mother's death in 1958.

Mary Meigs divides her time between Montreal and Kingsbury, Quebec.
Festival 11 (1993)

HOMINY GRITS BREAD

This recipe was given to me by Hortense Flexner, whose poetry was translated into French by Marguerite Yourcenar.

2 cups **milk**	1 tbsp **butter**
1/2 cup **Quaker hominy grits**	**salt**
2 **eggs,** beaten stiff	

- Put milk in saucepan, bring to a boil, stir in hominy and salt, continue stirring (about 10 minutes) until hominy is thick. Remove from stove, let cool a short time.
- Stir in butter, then beaten eggs, so that egg penetrates all.
- Pour into greased baking dish and bake at 375° F. for 30 minutes, or until brown on top.

BOEUF STROGONOFF

I thought you might be interested in this recipe for Boeuf Strogonoff that Mary McCarthy gave me in the late '50s when we lived next door to each other on Cape Cod.

1 1/2 lbs **lean,tender beef**	1 tbsp **flour**
3 tbsp **lard**	1/2 cup **sour cream**
1 **onion,** minced	**salt and pepper**
1 tbsp **tomato paste**	**mushrooms,** sliced (optional)
1 cup **beef stock**	

- Have the butcher cut the steak as thin as possible, less than 1/2 inch thick. Then cut it in strips one inch wide, four inches long. Pat with salt and pepper and put aside three to four hours.
- Melt lard in frying pan, add onion; when onion begins to cook, add tomato paste and the steak. Simmer 20 minutes.
- Remove meat, work in flour, return meat and add stock. Cook 10 more minutes uncovered and then add cream.
- Sliced mushrooms may be added with stock.
- OR the meat and the onion can be browned separately over a quick fire, while a sauce is being made of the other ingredients. The meat is then added to the sauce and cooked for 10 minutes. When using this method, use 2 tablespoons of butter and 2 tablespoons of flour to thicken the sauce.

KEN MITCHELL

Kenneth Mitchell began his writing career with the novel **Wandering Rafferty** (Macmillan) in 1972; since then he has published 18 books including novels, short story collections and poetry, although the bulk of his work has been written for the stage and film.

He was born and educated in Saskatchewan and is now on the faculty of the University of Regina. In addition, he has been the Scottish-Canadian Exchange Fellow at Edinburgh University and visiting professor of English at the University of Nanjing in China. During 1986-7 he taught at the Foreign Affairs College in Beijing.

His play **Gone the Burning Sun** was inspired by the life of Norman Bethune, the controversial Canadian doctor who became a hero to the Chinese. First produced at the Guelph Festival in 1984, it won the Canadian Authors Association award for Best Canadian Play and was nominated for the Governor General's Award. Since then he has taken his play across Canada, and to Australia, Germany, Ireland and China. It has been published several times, most recently in **Rebels in Time** (NeWest Press), a collection of 3 Mitchell plays including the historical dramas **Davin, the Politician and The Great Cultural Revolution**.

Among Ken Mitchell's other plays are the musical production **Cruel Tears** (Talonbooks, 1977; **The Shipbuilder** (Fifth House, 1990); the stage and television play **Chautauqua Girl** (Playwrights Canada, 1982); **All Our Yesterdays**, produced in 1986; **Melody Farm** (1987); and the one-man drama **Tommy** (1986), based on the life of the CCF-NDP leader Tommy Douglas. He wrote **The Great Electrical Revolution, Saskatchewan Suite**, and the Genie-winning **The Hounds of Notre Dame** as film scripts for the National Film Board.

Among his works of literary criticism is **Sinclair Ross: A Reader's Guide** (Coteau, 1984). **Through the Nan Da Gate: A China Journey** (Thistledow, 1986), Ken Mitchell's first collection of poetry, grew out of his year in China 1980-81. The poems in **Witches & Idiots** (Nightwood, 1990) reflect his deep love of the prairie landscape. In 1993 Ken Mitchell returned to novel-writing with **Stones of the Dalai Lama** (Greystone/Douglas & McIntyre).

Festival 7 (1989) and 10 (1992)

HAZELNUT CHEESECAKE

For a special dessert with an indescribable texture and an unforgettable taste, try this recipe for hazelnut cheesecake, obtained from Chicago.

1 1/2 cups **shelled hazelnuts**	1/2 cup **heavy cream**
butter	4 **eggs**
1/3 cup **graham cracker crumbs**	1 3/4 cups **sugar**
2 lbs **cream cheese**	1 tsp **vanilla**

- Toast hazelnuts at 400° F until crisp. Rub off the skins and grind the nuts to powder.
- Butter metal cake pan, roughly 8" x 8"x 3" deep, and sprinkle with graham cracker crumbs.
- Blend cream cheese, eggs, cream, sugar, vanilla in an electric mixer. Add nuts last.
- Spread this mixture over the graham cracker crumbs, and set the pan into a slightly larger pan filled to 1/2" with boiling water. Bake for two hours at 300° F.
- After two hours, turn oven off and let cake sit for one hour.
- Lift pan out of water, place on rack, let stand for two hours before serving.

SUSAN MUSGRAVE

The irrepressible poet, novelist, columnist, reviewer and non-fiction writer, Susan Musgrave, will tell you (should you care to ask) that she draws her inspiration from her experiences in public schools, psychiatric institutions and maximum security penitentiaries. She has been labelled an anti-feminist, an eco-feminist, the "JFK of the poetry world", and more frequently, the *enfant terrible* of Canadian letters. (She confesses that when she turned 40, she worried that critics would drop the *enfant* part; as far as she knows this hasn't happened.)

Susan Musgrave is the author of 13 books of poetry, the most recent being **Forcing the Narcissus** (McClelland & Stewart, 1994); **Kestrel and Leonardo** (Studio 123, 1990); **Cocktails at the Mausoleum** (McClelland & Stewart, 1985; revised edition, Beach Holme, 1992); and **Tarts and Muggers: Poems New and Selected** (McClelland & Stewart, 1982). **A Man to Marry, a Man to Bury** (McClelland & Stewart, 1979) was short-listed for the Governor General's Award. Another earlier book of poems, **Grave-Dirt and Selected Strawberries** (Macmillan, 1973) was short-listed for the same award.

Her novels are **The Charcoal Burners** (McClelland & Stewart, 1980), short-listed for the Seal First Novel Competition and the Governor General's Award; a children's novel, **Hag Head** (Clarke, Irwin & Co., 1980); and **The Dancing Chicken** (Methuen, 1987). Her collection of essays and columns, **Great Musgrave** (Prentice-Hall, 1989) was short-listed for the Stephen Leacock Award. Among the many periodicals and anthologies where her work may be found are **The New Canadian Poets 1970-1985** (McClelland & Stewart), **The Norton Introduction to Poetry, 3rd Edition** (1986), **The Norton Anthology of Modern Poetry** (1988 and 1989), *Exile, The Malahat Review, Event, Brick, Canadian Literature, Poetry Studies* and *Boundary 2* (U.S.), *Poetry Review* and *New Poetry* (Britain) and *Poetry Australia*

Susan Musgrave was writer in residence at the University of Waterloo from 1983 to 1985, and at the University of Western Ontario in 1992/93. She lives near Sidney, B.C

Festival 11 (1993) &
Workshop Summer 1987 and Fall 1993

AVOCADO, EGG AND CAVIAR PIE

Even loathers of caviar (like myself) find this hors d'oeuvre addictive.

1 **large avocado** (or 2 small ones)
3 tbsp **purple onion**
6 **eggs, hard-boiled**
3 tbsp **Mississippi Honey Mustard Mayonnaise (or plain mayonnaise)**
3 1/2 oz jar **lumpfish caviar** (the cheap whale-friendly kind, around $4.00!)

- Mash avocado and press in 8" or 9" glass pie plate.
- Chop purple onion finely and sprinkle over avocado.
- Chop hard-boiled eggs very finely and combine with Honey Mustard Mayonaise or plain mayonnaise. Spread gently over the onion layer.
- Spoon caviar on top of egg and mayonnaise layer.
- Chill and serve with TableWater biscuits or sesame seed crackers.

GRILLED PACIFIC NORTHWEST SALMON

The only salmon I've eaten that comes close to this one was Honeyed Peppered Smoked Sockeye at a potlatch in Skidegate on Haida Gwaii (Queen Charlotte Islands). You can eat this every night (we did, summer of 1993!) and still want more.

1/2 cup **unsalted butter**
1/3 cup **honey**
1/3 cup **brown sugar**
2 tbsp **freshly squeezed lemon juice**
1 tsp **natural liquid smoke flavouring**

3/4 tsp **crushed dried red pepper flakes**
pinch of **allspice** (optional)
2 lbs **salmon fillets, skin on,** in 2 pieces (4 portions)

- Combine butter, honey, brown sugar, lemon juice, liquid smoke, red pepper flakes, and allspice, if desired, in a saucepan. Cook over medium heat, stirring, for about 5 minutes or until smooth. Cool to room temperature.
- Arrange the salmon in a dish just large enough to hold it. Pour the cooled marinade over it and let it stand for 15 minutes. Turn, baste with marinade and let stand for another 15 minutes.
- Prepare hot coals for grilling (or gas barbecue, etc.)
- Oil the grill well and cook the salmon, skin side up, over medium heat for five to seven minutes. Turn and cook until fish flakes easily, another five to seven minutes.
- Transfer fish to a platter and serve immediately.
- Natural hickory smoke flavour is one ingredient you may not have on hand, but—for the sake of this recipe alone—it's well worth purchasing. You use very little at a time so a bottle is likely to last years. Ingredients (I was worried so I checked) include water, natural hickory smoke flavour, vinegar and brown sugar.

KNOWLTON NASH

Knowlton Nash began his distinguished career as a journalist in 1946 with a job as a sports reporter for the *Globe and Mail*; he moved to British United Press the following year as a reporter and editor. From 1951 to 1958 he was Director of Information for the International Federation of Agricultural Producers in Washington, D.C., leaving that post to become a freelance correspondent, using Washington as his base and travelling on assignment to virtually every corner of the world. He returned to Canada in early 1969 to become the CBC's director of television news and current affairs. Canadians, however, came to know Knowlton Nash best when he became the news anchor on CBC television's *The National* in 1978, a position he relinquished to Peter Mansbridge in 1988 in order to become the corporation's senior correspondent.

His books include **History On The Run** (1984), a memoir which covers his years as a foreign correspondent. The history of news broadcasting in Canada is told in his book **Prime Time At Ten**. He wrote the real story behind the Canada-U.S. "cold war" of 1961-63 and the personal conflict between the two countries' leaders in **Kennedy & Diefenbaker: Fear and Loathing Across the Undefended Border** (McClelland & Stewart, 1990).

Although he retired from his job as CBC's senior correspondent in November 1992, Knowlton Nash continues to host CBC's *Witness* documentary series and *Newsworld's* weekly retrospective of major news stories, *Sense of History*. He also teaches journalism at the University of Regina and is at work on a comprehensive history of Canadian broadcasting that will be published by McClelland & Stewart in 1994.

Festival 6 (1988)

KNOWLTON'S OATMEAL COOKIES

I've concentrated all my creative cookery into this one recipe—Quality over Quantity!

1 1/2 cups **flour**   1 1/2 cups **brown sugar**
2 cups **oatmeal**   1 tsp **vanilla**
1 tsp **salt**   1 tsp **baking soda**
3/4 cup **coconut**   1/4 cup **boiling water**
1 cup **butter**

- Mix flour, oatmeal, salt and coconut together.
- Dissolve baking soda in boiling water.
- Blend together butter, brown sugar, vanilla and the baking soda/boiling water mixture.
- Blend dry ingredients into the butter and sugar mixture.
- Drop by spoonfuls onto greased pan and pat flat with a cold spoon.
- Bake in a 350° - 400°F oven 6 - 10 minutes.

P. K. PAGE

Patricia Kathleen Page was born in England and came to Canada in 1919. Since then she has lived in many parts of this country—as a sales clerk and actress in New Brunswick, a filing clerk and historical researcher in Montreal, and script writer for the NFB in Ottawa. After her marriage to W. Arthur Irwin, she lived in Brazil, Mexico and Australia.

Her writing career began in 1935 with the publication of her first poem in the London (England) *Observer.* Her subsequent work includes the novel **The Sun and The Moon** (Macmillan, 1944; republished with other fiction by Anansi in 1973); **As Ten As Twenty** (poems, Ryerson, 1946); **The Metal and the Flower** (McClelland & Stewart, 1954), the book of poems which won her the Governor General's Award; **Cry Ararat! Poems New and Selected** (McClelland & Stewart, 1967); **Poems (1942-1973) Selected and New** (Anansi, 1974); **Evening Dance of the Grey Flies** (poetry and prose, Oxford, 1981); and **The Glass Air** (poetry, drawings and essays, Oxford, 1985), a selection of work from the early 1940s.

During her years in Brazil (1960-1963), she kept a journal and began drawing and painting. Her journal, illustrated by the sketches she made, became the B.C. Book Prize winner **Brazilian Journal**, published in 1987 by Lester & Orpen Dennys. It was also short-listed for the Governor General's non-fiction award.

P.K. Page's most recent books have been in the field of children's literature. **A Flask of Sea Water** (1989) is an original fairy tale about a young goatherd who must journey to the ocean which he has never seen to bring back a flask of seawater in order to win the hand of a princess. **The Travelling Musicians** (Kids Can Press, 1991), originally commissioned by the Victoria Symphony to accompany a Murray Adaskin composition, is based on the Grimm's fairy tale *The Musicians of Bremen*. **Wisdom from Nonsense Land** (Porcepic, 1991) is a collection of verses written by her father from France during the first World War.

P.K. Page became an Officer of the Order of Canada in 1977, won the CAA Literary Award for Poetry in 1985-6, and holds honorary doctorates from the Universities of Victoria and British Columbia. Her forthcoming books are **The Goat That Flew** (Beach Holme, 1994), a sequel to **A Flask of Seawater**, and a book of poetry, **Hologram** (Brick, 1994).

Festival 6 (1988)

SHRIMP MARIA STUART

2 cups **cooked shrimp**	1 tbsp **potato flour**
1/2 cup **butter**	1/4 cup **parsley,** chopped
1 small glass **brandy**	4 tbsp **tomato ketchup**
1 1/2 cups **cream**	1 tsp **worcestershire sauce**

- Sautee shrimp in butter. Add brandy. Light it. When flames die, stir in cream thickened with potato flour. Add parsley, ketchup and worcestershire sauce.
- Don't overcook. Shrimp are delicate.

RICE SALAD

4 cups **cooked rice** (wild is the most delicious but long-grain brown or a mixture is fine)	1/4 cup **fresh mint,** chopped
	4 **scallions,** thinly sliced
	1/4 cup **olive oil**
1 cup **shelled pecan halves**	1/3 cup **orange juice**
1 cup **yellow raisins**	1 1/2 tsp **salt**
grated rind of 1 large orange	**black pepper, freshly ground**

- Toss gently. Let stand two hours for flavors to develop.
- Serve at room temperature.
- Serves 6 - 8

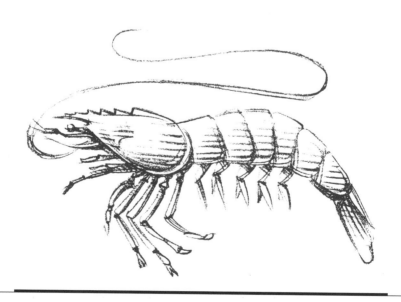

PASS & KISHKAN

The poetry writing career of John Pass began in 1971 with **Taking Place** (Talonbooks). Since then he has published nine more books of poetry including **Love's Confidence** (Caledonia, 1976), **There Go The Cars** (Sesame Press, 1979) and **An Arbitrary Dictionary** (Coach House, 1984), described by *Canadian Literature* as ". . .an absolute delight. A rare delight."

In 1992 John Pass's 10th book of poetry **The Hour's Acropolis** (Harbour) was nominated for the B.C. Book Prizes' Dorothy Livesay Poetry Award. *Books in Canada* called it "one of the finest books of the year" and "a prime example of what fine-tuned poetry can accomplish.

John Pass's poem, "Actaeon" won the 1988 Canada Poetry Prize; the poem was read on CBC's *Morningside*, published in *Books in Canada* and in **The Hour's Acropolis** as "Names". John Pass has taught English at Capilano College for the past nineteen years.

For much of her poetry, Theresa Kishkan draws from moments in her own life. Originally from Vancouver Island, she spent a year living off the west coast of Ireland, then travelled through Europe, stopping to live in Greece for six months. For the past 11 years she has lived with her family near Ruby Lake on the Sunshine Coast of British Columbia; here she and her husband, John Pass, publish chapbooks on a one hundred and ten year old Chandler & Price printing press which they have lovingly restored. Their printing partnership is known as High Ground Press.

She wrote her first book of poetry, **Arranging the Gallery** (Fiddlehead) in 1976; her second, **Ikons of the Hunt** (Sono Nis) was published in 1978. Then came a period of starting a family, building a house and making gardens. Believing that by concentrating on the particular the poet can access the universal elements of literature, Theresa Kishkan has used such things as the mysteries of pregnancy and childbirth, and her son's discovery of tadpoles in the poems in her most recent collection, **Black Cup** (Beach Holme, 1993). She is also the author of two chapbooks, **I Thought I Could See Africa** (High Ground, 1991) and **Morning Glory** (Reference West, 1991) which won the bp nichol Prize for the best chapbook in English published in Canada in 1991.

Festival 7 (1989) & Workshops Spring 1989

THE CRUST

2 tsp **Fermipan yeast**
4 cups **unbleached flour** (or 3 cups unbleached flour and 1 cup whole wheat flour)
pinch salt
1 1/2 cups **cold water**
1/4 cup **olive oil**

- Put the yeast, flour and salt in the bowl of food processor fitted with dough blade. Pulse several times to mix.
- With machine running, add cold water and olive oil through feed tube, and mix until dough forms a ball.
- Finish kneading by hand on a floured board, adding a little more flour if dough is too sticky.
- Let rise in oiled bowl in a warm place until dough has doubled in size, about one hour.
- Divide dough into four sections and press the air bubbles out of each section. Using your hands or a rolling pin on a lightly floured surface, shape each section into a round. Let the rounds rest on an oiled pizza pan or on a board sprinkled with cornmeal if you're going to bake the pizzas on a stone. Cover lightly with a towel and let rise for 20 to 30 minutes.
- Preheat oven to 400° F. If you're using a pizza stone, put it in the oven to preheat as well. (It takes a stone about 30 minutes to heat sufficiently.) Just before placing the pizzas on it, sprinkle it with a little cornmeal. Top the pizzas and bake for 15 to 20 minutes.

TOPPINGS:

- Puree 5 or 6 sun-dried tomatoes with a little olive oil and a clove or two of garlic. Brush this on the dough and then top with sliced new potatoes which you've steamed until they're just tender. Sprinkle a little parmesan cheese on top or even a little gorgonzola.
- Brush the dough with a little olive oil (this prevents the crust from getting soggy) and strew with thinly sliced smoked salmon (the barbecued tips, which are quite reasonably priced, taste just fine!), lightly sauteed mushrooms (pine mushrooms in late fall taste sublime with the smoked salmon. . .), green onions, chopped parsley and cubes of mozzarella cheese or monterey jack with jalapenos.

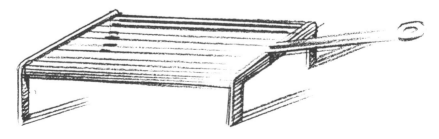

- Make a pesto sauce of 2 cups of fresh basil leaves, 1/2 cup of olive oil, 2 tbsp. pine nuts, 2 cloves of garlic, and 1/2 cup of parmesan cheese blended in a food processor or blender until smooth. Spoon about 1/2 cup of this onto a pizza shell, saving the rest of the sauce for pasta or whatever. Slice 3 or 4 fully ripe Roma tomatoes over the pesto, dot the top with cubes of mozzarella cheese.
- Brush the shell with a little olive oil, add 4 or 5 cloves of thinly sliced garlic, a handful each of chopped fresh sage, rosemary and parsley, some good olives (like Nicoise or Ligurian), and dapple the top with cheese, mozzarella or provolone.

This would make a nice light lunch for four people, each pizza being quartered so that everyone could have a slice of each kind. Or else each pizza could be cut into thin wedges for an antipasto or hors d'oeuvre table.

HERBED CHEESE BREAD

3 tsp **Fermipan yeast**	l cup **fresh herbs,** chopped
3 1/2 cups **unbleached flour**	(**parsley and rosemary** are nice)
l cup **oat bran** (or wheat bran if preferred)	1 1/2 cups **cold water**
1/2 tsp **salt**	2 **eggs,** lightly beaten
1/2 cup **parmesan cheese**	3 tbsp **olive oil**

- Put yeast, flour, bran, salt, cheese and herbs in the bowl of the food processor fitted with dough blade. Pulse a few times to mix.
- With motor running, add water, eggs, and oil, mixing until dough forms a ball.
- Finish kneading the dough on a lightly floured board, adding more flour if needed.
- Put dough into an oiled bowl and cover with a cloth. Let rise in a warm place until doubled, about 1 1/2 hours.
- Punch down and divide dough in half, forming each half into a loaf, either oblong or round.
- If you're using a baking stone, let the loaves rise on a board sprinkled with cornmeal.
- If you're using baking sheets, oil them lightly and place dough on them.
- Either way, cover with a towel and let rise until doubled, about an hour.
- Bake in a preheated 425° F oven for about 30 minutes. Spray the loaves 2 or 3 times with water for a good crust. If you use a baking stone, preheat it in the oven for 30 minutes; remember to sprinkle it with cornmeal before placing the loaves on it.
- Variation: This bread is nice with the addition of 1/3 cup of chopped sun-dried tomatoes, substituting their oil for olive oil.

KIT PEARSON

Children's writer and former librarian Kit Pearson is the author of five childrens' novels, all published by Penguin Books Canada. Her first, **The Daring Game** was published in 1986. A year later **A Handful of Time** won the Canadian Library Association's Book of the Year for Children Award.

The **Sky is Falling** (1989), is the first novel of a trilogy about two British children—ten-year-old Norah and her five-year-old brother Gavin—who are evacuated to Canada during World War II. It won the Canadian Library Association's Book of the Year for Children Award, Mr. Christie's Book Award and the Geoffrey Bilson Award for Historical Fiction for Young People. In **Looking at the Moon** (1991), the second of the series, the children are three years older and Norah is enmeshed in the misery of puberty. **The Lights Go On Again** (1993) concentrates on Gavin, now age ten and full of apprehension about having to go back to England at the war's end.

Her retelling of a French-Canadian folktale in **The Singing Basket** (Groundwood, 1990) tells the story of the punishment of greed and deceit; it was illustrated by Ann Blades.

Kit Pearson took her degree in Librarianship from the University of B.C. and her M.A. from the Simmons College Centre for the Study of Children's Literature in Boston. She worked as a children's librarian in Ontario and British Columbia for 10 years and now writes full time, supported by stints of teaching writing for children and children's literature.

Festival 6 (1988) & Workshops Spring 1992

ALBERTA DUCKS

Wild ducks (cleaned and plucked)
Onions
Bacon slices
Orange juice

- Wash ducks, pulling out any leftover innards and pinfeathers. Dry thoroughly.
- Put half or whole onion in each duck, depending on size.
- Place ducks breast up in roasting pan and lay a slice of bacon across each. Cover with foil and roast 3 hours in 325°F oven.
- Uncover for last 3/4 hour and baste with orange juice.
- Ducks can sit in 200°F oven covered with foil until ready to serve. Serve with red currant jelly, applesauce, or orange sauce.

MAPLE MOUSSE

3/4 cup **maple syrup**
1 tbsp **gelatin**
2 **egg whites**

1/2 pint **whipping cream**
1 tbsp **sherry**

- Boil maple syrup for one minute.
- Dissolve gelatin in a little cold water and add to syrup. Stir until gelatin dissolved but do not boil.
- Chill until beginning to thicken, then blend in beaten egg whites and whipped cream.
- Add sherry and chill.

NINO RICCI

Toronto writer Nino Ricci was born in Ontario to parents from the Molise region of Italy, attended York University and taught English at a secondary school in Nigeria under the auspices of CUSO. In 1987 he completed an M.A. in Creative Writing at Concordia University where he subsequently taught creative writing and Canadian literature. Recently he spent a year studying Italian literature at the University of Florence, Italy.

His first novel, **Lives of the Saints** (Cormorant 1990), has been described as "a gem of a novel", "a rich and wonderful tapestry", and "a novel of remarkable beauty and unforgetable power". The story of the immigration to Canada of a seven-year-old Italian boy, Vittorio Innocente, and his mother, it won the Governor General's Award for Fiction, the W.H. Smith Books in Canada First Novel Award, and the F.G. Brassani Prize for Fiction. It was published in Britain by W.H. Allen Co. (winning two prestigious British prizes) and in the United States by Alfred A. Knopf as **The Book of Saints**. Rights for French, Swedish, German, Danish, Japanese and Spanish editions have also been sold.

The sequel to **Lives of the Saints** was published in 1993 by McClelland & Stewart. **In a Glass House** resumes the story of Vittorio Innocente's life from the death of his mother enroute to Canada to his first job as a teacher in west Africa.

Nino Ricci's short fiction has appeared in *The Fiddlehead, The Moosehead Anthology, Writ, Saturday Night* and in *Rocordi*, the anthology published by Guernica Editions. His articles and reviews have appeared in *The Canadian Journal of Political and Social Theory*, the Toronto *Star*, and *Books in Canada*. He is a member of the Board of Directors of the Canadian Centre of International P.E.N.

Festival 9 (1991)

ALL-PURPOSE PASTA ALLA PANNA

Speed of preparation, ease of synchronization of constituent elements, and minimum messing of cooking utensils make this meal especially handy for serving dinner guests you'd forgotten you'd invited. Its many possible variations (as many as 7 to the power of 12, depending on the number of ingredients at your disposal) can help provide blander diets with the important illusion of constant change, with negligible expense of either creativity or exertion.

PRE-COOKING PREPARATION:
- Open the fridge.
- Determine which of the following items you possess and place them on kitchen counter: cream, milk, margarine, butter, cream cheese, blue cheese, parmesan cheese, havarti cheese, fresh mushrooms, frozen peas, onions (if you keep them in the fridge), garlic (ditto), cooked ham, spicy Genoa salami, frankfurters.
- Open kitchen cupboards.
- Determine which of following items you possess and place them on kitchen counter: oregano, basil, garlic salt, Campbell's mushroom soup, canned peas, hot sauce, dried chili peppers, chili powder, black pepper, curry powder, olive oil, worcestershire sauce, soy sauce.
- Decide on the most feasible combination of available ingredients for the formation of your sauce, aiming for lateral variation (i.e. cream or milk as a base and then one cheese, one meat, etc.).
- Promptly return other items to their proper places.
- Remove your ever-present, quick-cooking fresh/frozen pasta of choice from the freezer, or, if you have six or seven hours to spare, make your own.
- Remove the following items from your cupboards: one large pot, one not-so-large pot, a wooden spoon, a plastic pasta scoop, a pasta strainer. No other cooking utensils should be used.

COOKING:
- Set the pasta water to heat in the large pot. Note that the time it takes for the water to come to a boil (10 - 15 minutes) and the pasta to cook (3 - 5 minutes) should equal exactly the time you take to prepare the sauce. This requires considerable practise, so beginners may wish to set the water at only medium heat.
- Slit open the fresh/frozen pasta's plastic packaging and set the package near the pot of heating water to allow the pasta to thaw. You will need about 125 grams of pasta per person; if you are serving guests add another 100—150 grams per person to avoid the humiliation of appearing less than excessive.

(Continued on pg. 104)

• Begin the sauce. There is no standard procedure here, though generally I proceed thus:

SAUCE:

• Melt ample amounts of butter or margarine in the not-so-large pot.
• Add anything that needs to be fried, for example mushrooms, onion, garlic, and fry until fried.
• Pour in cream or milk. A cup or so will do for now; you can stir in more later as needed to thin the sauce.
• Stir in your cheese of choice, grated or in slices or chunks. If you are using cream cheese you will need another sweeter cheese to offset its basically unpleasant taste.
• Add in your meat of choice, cut into small squares.
• Season to taste.
• NOTE: In every instance it is important that you clean up any mess you make as you go.
• Let the sauce cook until it is done. This should occur a minute or so after you have finished cooking and draining the pasta.

The entire procedure, from start to finish, should take just under 25 minutes and should leave you with kitchen counters clean and with essentially one dirty pot. (The pasta pot cannot really be said to be dirty, after all, and could even be left on the stove to be re-used as is the following evening).

Before serving, assign the dish a name; this will impress your guests. The easiest method is simply to translate all ingredients into Italian; i.e. fettuccine with two cheeses, mushrooms, and cream would be fettuccine con formaggi e funghi alla panna. Use of one's Christian name is also a favoured method, as in spaghettini Bob or linguine Francine.

VERA ROSENBLUTH

"It's often not until a parent or grandparent dies that we realize just how little we know about our family history," says Vera Rosenbluth who was fascinated as a child by her own grandparents' stories.

Born in Ottawa in 1946, Vera Rosenbluth earned a B.A. at U.B.C. in 1967, studied at L'Universite d'Aix-en-Provence, France, in 1967-68 and returned to the University of B.C. to take an M.A. in comparative literature in 1971. After studying and travelling, she began her career as a professional writer and broadcaster.

Much of her work has been at CBC radio where she started with the Vancouver morning show in 1972. Her radio credits include many documentaries dealing with social and historical issues: programs about women's issues; several programs made with tape collected on a 1972 trip to China; *Following the Rainbow*, a drama-documentary about the *Komagata Maru* incident; *To Dream of Flight*, a stereo sound feature; and *Official Secrets*, a drama-documentary about the Gouzenko spy trials. She has done several series for *Ideas*, among them a two-hour production *Through a Pathless Forest: The Brothers Grimm* (1985), another two-hour series *The Magic of Storytelling* (1986) and a three-hour series *The Mystery of Human Memory* (1988). She

also worked briefly in television, (1987 - 89) as senior researcher for *The Best Years*, the CBC's show for the over-50 set.

Awarded the 1971 CBC Oral History Award for *Women in B.C. Politics*, Vera Rosenbluth was also nominated for the 1988 Gabriel Award for *The Magic of Storytelling*. For *The Mystery of Human Memory*, she received honorable mention in the 25th Annual Major Armstrong Competition (1988) and was nominated for the Peabody and science writer awards (1989).

Her love of interviewing and gathering family stories led Vera Rosenbluth to operate her own business, Sound Portraits, from 1983 to 1987. A direct result of this enterprise was her book, **Keeping Family Stories Alive: A Creative Guide to Taping Your Family Life and Lore** (Hartley & Marks, 1990).

Currently, she and a partner operate *Links & Legacies*, a Vancouver-based company which helps families and organizations discover and preserve their history and stories using audiotape, videotape and print. As far as they know, *Links & Legacies* is unique in North America, offering workshops and programs as well as taped interviews that elicit the myriad stories of people's lives.
Festival 9 (1991)

As you know, my interest is in the area of family stories. Often recipes that have been passed on through the generations (the ones that have grease stains or chocolate smears on them!) do the same things that stories do: they make people feel connected, related, bound to each other. There's one particular dessert that my mother and I both make a lot, mainly because it's fast, versatile and delicious. It probably has a middle-European origin, but I've never seen it in a recipe book.

MIMI'S DRIBBLE CAKE

1/4 cup **soft margarine**	**fruit** (berries are great!)
3 tbsp **sugar**	3 tbsp **milk or cream**
2 **egg yolks**	3 tbsp **cottage cheese**
1 cup **flour**	**cinnamon**

- Combine margarine with 1 tbsp. sugar. Add 1 egg yolk and the flour, a little at a time. (Mixture will be a little crumbly.)
- Press on bottom of greased spring form pan.
- Cover with fruit (berries, sliced apples, sliced peaches or apricots, or any creative mixture of whatever's in season.)
- Combine in blender: 1 egg yolk, 2 tbsp sugar, 3 (generous) tbsp each of milk and cottage cheese, sprinkling of cinnamon. Pour over fruit.
- Bake at 375°F for 30 minutes.

Now, the only problem with this recipe is that you're left with 2 egg whites. So then you can always make a fruit pavlova!

FRUIT PAVLOVA

3 **egg whites** (at room temperature)	1 cup **whipping cream**
pinch **cream of tartar**	4 cups **strawberries, raspberries,**
3/4 cup **sugar**	**blueberries or peaches**
1 tsp **vanilla**	

- Beat egg whites with cream of tartar until soft peaks form. Beat in sugar one teaspoon at a time until stiff glossy peak form. Beat in vanilla.
- On a foil-lined baking sheet, spread meringue into a 10" circle, pushing up edge to form ring. Bake at 275°F for one and a half hours, or until firm to the touch. Turn off oven and leave meringue in oven to dry. Remove foil, let cool and place meringue on platter.
- Prepare fruit, slicing peaches or strawberries. Just before serving, spread whipped cream over meringue, then cover with fruit. Cut into pie-shaped wedges.

Of course, now the problem is, if you used two leftover egg whites from MIMI'S DRIBBLE CAKE, this time you are left with an extra egg yolk. My recommendation is to add it to your scrambled eggs the next morning!

LEEK AND CLAM SOUP

The other recipe I wanted to pass on is one for a soup. This one is so hearty that it is quite enough for a meal, particularly if you have some special bread to go with it. It's a family favourite after a day's skiing or hiking, or if everyone's too busy (or lazy) to cook more than soup.

2 cups minced **leeks**
1/4 cup each chopped **celery and onion**
2 cloves minced **garlic**
3 tbsp minced **carrot**
4 tbsp **margarine**
4 cups **beef stock**
1 1/2 cups **potatoes,** diced

2 - 7 1/2 oz cans **clams**
1 cup **milk**
salt and pepper
parsley, minced
garlic, minced
paprika

- Saute leeks, celery, onion, garlic and carrot in margarine until soft.
- Add stock and potatoes, cover, simmer until potatoes are tender.
- Puree in blender.
- Combine potato mixture with clams in large pot and add milk.
- Reheat (but do not boil).
- Season with salt, pepper.
- Garnish with parsley, minced garlic and paprika.
- Serves 8 (unless you have 2 hungry teenagers!)

CAROLE RUBIN

Carole Rubin graduated from York University in 1974 with an Honours degree in Fine Arts. Her focus shifted to environmental issues after moving to the Sunshine Coast of B.C. in 1980.

While working as a house-cleaner, arts coordinator, teacher, and caterer, Carole Rubin became a founding member and director of the B.C. Coalition for Alternatives to Pesticides in 1983, and subsequently helped to found and chair the B.C. and Canadian Environmental Networks' Pesticide Caucuses.

In 1988, Carole Rubin was appointed to the federal Priority Substances Panel which developed the first top 50 toxic substances "hit list" to be assessed under the Canadian Environmental Protection Act. Since 1989, she has been the coordinator of a national group of environmentalists working on ecological changes to Canada's pesticide legislation.

Carole Rubin's first two books were released in 1989: **How to Get Your Lawn and Garden Off Drugs**, first published by Friends of the Earth, and **The Organic Approach to Home Gardening,** published by the Ontario Ministry of Environment. She has written articles for *Harrowsmith* (July/August 1989), *Canadian Living Magazine* (May 1991), and a weekly column, "Earthwords and Eco-tips", on a range of environmental issues for a local newspaper, *The Leader*. (November 1990-October 1991)

Her public addresses include "The Power of One", which was broadcast in part 5 of David Suzuki's CBC radio series *A Matter of Survival*, July 1989; "You Can Get Your Industry Off Drugs", a speech to the 17th Annual Horticultural Industry Days in Winnipeg, November 1989, and television segments on CBC's *Down to Earth* (November 1990), and *Marketplace* (December 1992).

Carole Rubin is s Director of the West Coast Environmental Law Association, and a Steering Committee member of the Pesticide Action Network, North America. She lives near Sechelt, B.C., where she lets her yard go native, and grows organic vegetables. She is at work on her next book, **How to Get Your Lawn Off Grass**.

Festival 8 (1990)

LENTIL THYME SOUP

This recipe produces a soup so hearty that it is really a stew. The dish improves with age, as do most stews, and takes on a real "comfort food" consistency and flavour as the texture thickens with cooking.

Use fresh organic carrots, tomatoes, celery, and garlic from your garden, or purchase them at a store that carries organic produce. The flavour is not the only thing that will benefit; so will you, your children, pets, the soil, our water, farmworkers, etc.

Tomato paste and canned tomatoes have the highest pesticide residues of all foods, except raisins, so go organic!

Tomato tip: you can use frozen tomatoes from the garden in this recipe. Freeze them without blanching, 6 to a bag, and add directly from the freezer to this soup whenever the mood strikes.

6 cups **raw organic lentils**	**fresh black pepper** to taste
13 - 14 cups **water**	4 tbsp **dry sherry**
1 tsp **salt**	4 tbsp **fresh lemon juice**
6 - 8 cloves **organic garlic**, minced	3 tbsp **molasses**
2 medium **onions**, chopped	2 tbsp **wine or cider vinegar**
4 stalks **organic celery**, chopped	1 tbsp **thyme** (or more to taste)
6 medium **organic carrots**, chopped	1 tsp **oregano**
6 medium **organic tomatoes**, chopped	

- Rinse the lentils well, and add to a BIG soup pot with the water and salt. Bring to a gentle boil, then cover and simmer on lowest heat, for 3 - 4 hours. Stir occasionally, and add water as necessary.
- Saute the minced garlic, chopped onion, carrot and celery together in a large fry pan with a bit of oil or butter, and add to the lentils at the 3 - 4 hour mark. Cover, and continue to simmer, low heat, for another 30 - 60 minutes.
- Add the remaining ingredients to the pot at least 30 minutes before serving, stir through, and cover the pot again.

As a soup, before dinner, makes 8 - 12 servings. As a main dish with hearty bread and perhaps a salad, makes 6 - 10 servings. Can be frozen in smaller portions for later use.

BRAZILIAN BLACK BEAN SOUP

Not too hot, this soup is great for a dinner party. The bright colours of orange, green, and red with the black beans makes this an attractive dish. Needless to say, organic produce and beans should be used.

2 cups **dry black beans**
3 1/2 cups **water**

Group A:
1 cup chopped **onion**
3 cloves **garlic,** crushed
1 large **carrot,** sliced thin
1 stalk **celery,** chopped
1 cup **green pepper,** chopped
1 tsp **ground coriander**
1 1/2 tsp **ground cumin**
2 tbsp **canola oil**

Group B:
2 **oranges,** peeled and sectioned and seeded
1/2 cup **orange juice**
1/4 tsp **black pepper, freshly ground**
1/4 tsp **dry red peppers**
1/2 tsp **fresh lemon juice**
1 tbsp **dry sherry**

- Rinse the beans well, place in a deep bowl, and cover with water to at least an inch above the beans. Let soak for a minimum of 4 hours. Pour off excess water, and place beans in a soup pot with the 3 1/2 cups of water. Bring to gentle boil, cover, and simmer at very low heat for 1 1/2 hours.
- Saute group A, beginning with onions and garlic, in the oil. Add the rest of group A, and saute until vegetables are soft and spicy. Add mixture to beans, and let soup continue to simmer, at lowest heat for 1/2 - 3/4 hour.
- Add group B to soup. Stir thoroughly, cover, and allow to simmer for 1/2 hour. Taste, and adjust seasoning, adding more dry red pepper to give it heat. If you want a thicker soup, remove a cup of the mix, puree it in the blender, and return it to the pot. Add more water to make it thinner.

This recipe can be doubled for larger groups. Each dish can be topped with sour cream or yogurt when served, but I eat it just as is.

HOLLEY  RUBINSKY

"What's at the heart of my writing is getting inside another head," writes Holley Rubinsky. "What I'm aiming for is condensed feeling, a crystallization of a moment. What I want is to craft without losing passion." And in her debut collection of short stories, **Rapid Transits and Other Stories** (Polestar Press, 1990), she certainly accomplished her goal, especially when it came to getting inside the head of her major character, Harriet Mary Dawn.

Since it was originally published in *The Malahat Review*, the title story of her book—described by William French of the *Globe and Mail* as "a ribald, haunting story"—won the 1988 Gold Medal for Fiction in the National Magazine Awards and the inaugural $10,000 McClelland & Stewart Journey Prize, financed in part by the Canadian royalties to James Michener's novel **Journey**.

Although **Rapid Transits** was her first published book, her early work appeared in *Redbook, Redbook's Famous Fiction, Woman's Own* (England) and *McCall's*, while her more recent stories have appeared in *Prairie Fire, Event, Descant, Canadian Fiction, Prism International* and *The Malahat Review*."Preacher's Geese", published in *The Malahat Review*, was a finalist in the 1988 Western Magazine Awards. Her stories have also been published in **The Macmillan Anthology I**, **The Journey Prize Anthology I**, and **Fictions II** which was published in 1993 by Second Story Press.

Holley Rubinsky grew up in southern California. She was educated at UCLA, where in 1965 she won the UCLA Samuel Goldwyn Writing Award. In 1975 she came to teach in Kaslo in British Columbia's Kootenay district. Today she divides her time between Kaslo and Toronto. She has begun work on a novel, **Road's End** and is now a practitioner of the Usui (Reiki) System of Natural Healing.

Festival 9 (1991)

The trouble with eating at home is that it usually involves cooking. Cooking involves baking, barbequing, boiling, braising, broiling, browning: and that's just some of the *B*s. (The process gets really exhausting at the *S*s when the cook may be required to scald, scallop, shred, smother, stir-fry and stuff.) The home cook must be chef, sous-chef, scullery maid, sommelier, bartender, server, busboy and sometimes, dishwasher. This does not take into account the hunting and gathering aspect of meal preparation. Or the time-consuming chase for the one elusive-but-essential ingredient.

In Kaslo, British Columbia, reside some of the best cooks west of the Rockies. What the clever maitre d'home here does is throw a party to celebrate something. In the old days these friendly events were called potlucks, and still are.

GORDON'S BEDEVILLED CHICKEN CURRY

Note: Best made a day or two ahead. Amounts are "per chicken", either cut-up or else 4 - 5 legs and thighs. Chicken is skinned, with fat removed.

1 **whole chicken,** cut up	1 **over-ripe banana,** sliced
4 **medium onions,** chopped	1 piece **kafir lime skin**, soaked and minced
1 can **coconut milk**	(optional)
1 tbsp **garlic,** minced or sliced	4 tbsp **olive oil**
1 tbsp **fresh ginger,** minced or sliced	1 tbsp **sesame oil**
2-4 tbsp **Asian curry powder**	8 **medium fresh mushrooms,** quartered

• Saute onions in combined oils with ginger and garlic until tender.
• Add coconut milk, kafir (if you have it), curry powder and banana.
• Bring to boil, simmer 10 minutes.
• Add leg, thigh and wing sections.
• Bring to boil again, cover, simmer one hour.
• Cube breast meat and add with mushrooms.
• Simmer another 30 minutes.
• Serve over aromatic Thai rice or basmati rice. To be accompanied by numbingly cold beer or very dry white wine.

JEANNIE'S FRUIT CREAM DESSERT

2 cups **plain yoghurt**	1/2 cup **sugar**
2 cups **sour cream**	1/2 cup **crushed pineapple,** drained
1 tsp **vanilla**	2 tbsp **raw almond slices**

• Stir and chill, sprinkle with extra pineapple and almonds. Recipe can be doubled.

PAUL S T. PIERRE

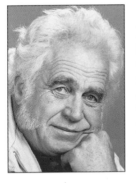

P aul St. Pierre has been many things in his time. He served as the Liberal MP for the Coast Chilcotin riding from 1968 to 1972, a post which included two years as parliamentary secretary in the external affairs department, a stint as delegate to the United Nations, and chairmanship of the B.C. Liberal caucus from 1970 to 1972. He was a police commissioner for the province of B.C. from 1979 to 1983 and a Vancouver *Sun* columnist. Currently, his weekly pieces appear in 20 B.C. newspapers.

Paul St. Pierre is one of Canada's greatest story tellers, and his writing is filled with the extraordinary stories of the ordinary people that he has met on his travels between his beloved Chilcotin country and Mexico, his part-time home. It was in the Chilcotin that he developed the award-winning CBC-TV series *Cariboo Country*. An early book which grew out of this series was **Breaking Smith's Quarter Horse** (1966), which reviewer Jamie Lamb calls "a flat-out masterpiece". The Smith stories, writes Lamb, "take a small cluster of people in a big, harsh, empty land and make them wonderfully interesting and important for people who would in the normal course of events have no interest in a place called Chilcotin."

In addition to **Smith's Quarter Horse**,

he wrote the play and the book, **Sister Balonika**, in 1969; **Chilcotin Holiday** (1970); **Smith and Other Events** (1983), which won the Western Writers of America Spur Award; **Boss of the Namko Drive** (1965) and **Chilcotin and Beyond** (Douglas & McIntyre, 1989).

His latest book, **In The Navel Of The Moon** (Douglas & McIntyre, 1993), set in Mexico, was published three years later than Paul St. Pierre intended because he had difficulty establishing the "voice" that he was looking for. But the book is worth the wait. In it, according to Jamie Lamb, he introduces the reader to a "handful of little people in a remote place and makes them interesting, funny and important. He views Mexico as a great stage, its inhabitants the cast of a grand old opera full of perverse passions and gestures."As in his books about the people of the Chilcotin, his love and understanding of the Mexican people are clearly shown. "Paul St. Pierre relays these stories beautifully," wrote the *New York Times* book reviewer, "in the language of the people and places he describes, the kind of vivid language that provides literature the nourishment it needs."
Festival 8 (1990)

CEVICHE, WET OR DRY

A standard fish dish of Mexico, usually treated as an appetizer. Oddly enough, in tourist towns such as Mazatlan, not one restaurant in twenty will admit ever hearing of fish ceviche. They will insist on serving you shrimp ceviche, which is not necessarily the best. In Mexican homes, fish ceviche is as common as Baked Beans in Boston and, as with beans, every home's preparation is slightly better than every other home's.

THE FISH

Although it is going to stand around for hours after you prepare it, nevertheless at the start the fish should be so fresh-caught that you still feel pity for it.

Most fish in the world are divided into delicate flavours (usually white such as ling cod, halibut or sole) and stronger flavours (salmon, mackerel, sturgeon). Only experimentation will decide which you prefer. Most people prefer the bland ones.

THE ONION

Big or green, all onions are acceptable.

THE JUICE FOR CURING

Fresh squeezed limes. No substitutes. There has never been a lemon hatched which compares with a lime. Do not even think about buying prepared lime juice in a bottle.

THE CHILIES

Nothing is more variable than people's taste for capsicum, the heating element of the hot chili peppers. So experiment. The popular view is that Mexicans only like peppers which can raise a blister on the forearm. That's not true. They use livelier peppers than we do, and so should your ceviche, but those who eat lava are usually just showing off.

Among the peppers: Jalapeno is usually favoured. Like tequila, it has a distinctive, lingering and pungent flavour. You can make sweet jelly with Jalapeno and still taste that distinctive tang. Tail of the Rat is hotter than Jalapeno and harder to find. The hottest of all peppers are not Mexican or South American but Jamaican, with perhaps some rivals from Southeast Asia and Hunan Province in China.

Go at it sensibly, remembering only that Ceviche is a dish of the tropics and like most of them, requires some internal fires lit in it.

PREPARATION

• Cube boneless fish fillets of your choice and, using a spoon, scoop out flesh from the back and other bones. Use no skin. Put two pounds of fish in a bowl and cover with a couple of cups of fresh undiluted lime juice for three to four hours. Stir from time to time to make sure all the fish is

being cured. Remember lime juice is, in effect, the stove on which you are cooking.
- Dice a large onion or chop green onions enough to fill a cup.
- Peel and then chop three large tomatoes. Chop, let's say, half a cup of Jalapenos.
- Half an hour before the first curing of the fish is completed, put the onion, tomato and Jalapeno into a bowl together with the following:
- Two cups of tomato juice
- Two cups of fresh squeezed lime juice;
- A teaspoon each of salt, white pepper and oregano; 4 tablespoons of white wine and the same of olive oil; half teaspoons of Tabasco and Worcestershire. Taste your mixture. You may find you want more of this or that. Add cilantro, tasting as you go. It is easy to add too much.
- Drain the bowl in which the fish was cured, rinse the fish pieces and transfer them to the Ceviche sauce.
- Refrigerate overnight. It's morning? Alright then, all day. The process takes 12 hours for good blending, even though your working time is less than 20 minutes.
- Serve with crackers or tostado chips on a plate with halved avocadoes on the side. (You may add the avocadoes to the ceviche if the entire dish is to be eaten at one sitting. If you plan to stretch out the ceviche for a bed time snack, leave out the avocadoes as they will turn black.)

DRY CEVICHE

Some prefer dry ceviche. I don't know why.
- For Dry, make the same bowl of ceviche sauce as above but without the tomato juice and with less olive oil. After it has stood 12 hours, remove the fish, place in a towel and squeeze out all liquid by wringing the towel. Abandon the sauce you laboured upon and eat the fish on crackers. Do not eat the towel. Sing *La Cucuracha*.

ANDREAS SCHROEDER

According to Andreas Schroeder (via La Rochefoucault), if youth is the time to try everything, and middle age the time to straighten out the resulting chaos, he must have arrived at middle age. "Several decades ago I was frantically writing in every genre invented, producing radio documentaries (CBC *Ideas*), directing films (**The Late Man, The Pub, Immobile**), founding and editing magazines (*Contemporary Literature in Translation, Canadian Fiction Magazine, Words from Inside*), writing weekly literary columns (The Vancouver *Province*), teaching creative writing (UBC, U-Vic, SSA, etc.), and hosting a weekly literary television show (*Synapse*). I raced motorcycles, parachuted out of small airplanes, lived with a bedouin tribe in the Baalbek (Lebanon) and served as Chairman of the Writers Union of Canada (1976-7)."

Today, Andreas Schroeder concentrates mostly on writing. His motorcycle rusts, his parachute moulders. "It's just me and my word processor," he says. "Occasionally I forget myself and commit cultural politics (for example, as founding chairman of the Public Lending Right Commission, 1985-8), but then I come back to my senses and return to writing once more. The pursuit of writing seems to require the longest apprenticeship in the world. Maybe that should bother me, but it doesn't."

Finalist for the 1977 Governor-General's Award for non-fiction and the 1984 Sealbooks First Novel Award, and winner of the 1990 Canadian Assoc. of Journalists' Top Investigative Journalism Award, Andreas Schroeder is the author of eleven books of fiction, non-fiction and docu-fiction. They include **The Ozone Minotaur** (Sono Nis, 1969), **File of Uncertainties** (Sono Nis, 1971), **The Late Man** (Sono Nis 1972), **Shaking It Rough** (Doubleday, 1976; Lorimer, 1979), **Toccata in 'D'** (Oolichan), **Dustship Glory** (Doubleday, 1986) and **The Mennonites** (Douglas & McIntyre, 1990). In 1990 he co-authored (with Jack Thiessen) a collection of "cheeky, satiric Mennonite Low-German short stories" entitled **The Eleventh Commandment** (Thistledown, 1990).

Andreas Schroeder is also the author of three volumes of poetry and three screenplays. His radio plays include a 5-part adaptation of his novel **Dustship Glory** for CBC's *Morningside*. He has published several hundred features in Canadian newspapers and magazines. His prose and poetry have appeared in more than 40 literary magazines and 30 anthologies in Canada, the U.S., the U.K., and Australia. He is also an editor and translator.

Festival 10 (1992) & Workshops Summer 1989, Fall 1992, Spring and Summer 1993

SCHROEDER'S SPECIAL

To tell you the truth, I'm such an inept cook that I can't come up with two recipes, but over the years I've refined and re-refined ONE recipe—a breakfast concoction known around here simply as "Schroeder's Special"—that may serve. Since I can at least guarantee you that it won't kill anyone, I'll pass it on.

2 **potatoes** for every 3 people
3 **eggs** for every 2 people
mozzarella cheese, grated
red or green peppers, onions, mushrooms, etc., diced

- Grease up a skittle and rasp up potatoes to the tune of approximately 2 potatoes for every 3 people. Dump into pan and fry until they're not quite done—still a bit sticky.
- Spread them evenly across the pan and break a few eggs (at least 3 for every 2 people) over them, being careful not to puncture the yokes.
- Scatter diced onions, peppers, mushrooms and whatever else strikes your fancy over the eggs. Then grate a generous sprinkling of the cheese across everything.
- Lower heat to a bit below medium (my stove's electric) and let everything bake a bit. Use the eggs to determine when it's done—they shouldn't be fried any more than the equivalent of sunny-side-up.

And there you have it—"Schroeder's Special". Always sets me up for one heckuva day!

CAROL SHIELDS

Carol Shields has staked out the lives of ordinary people as her writing territory and draws the readers of her seven novels, three volumes of short stories, and two poetry collections gently and with affectionate irony into the virtues, joys and griefs of everyday lives.

Ms. Shields began her novel-writing career in 1976 with **Small Ceremonies** which won the Canadian Authors' Association Award for best novel, and followed it within six years with **The Box Garden**, **Happenstance** and **A Fairly Conventional Woman**. Her 1987 novel **Swann: A Mystery** (Stoddart) won the Arthur Ellis Award for best Canadian crime novel, was shortlisted for the Governor General's Award, and became the December 1989 Quality Paperback Club selection. **The Republic of Love** (Random 1992) has been published in Canada, the U.S. and the U.K.

Her 1991 novel **A Celibate Season** (Coteau) was a collaboration with the Vancouver writer Blanche Howard.

Her books of short stories are: **Various Miracles** and **The Orange Fish** (Random House). Her published plays are **Departures and Arrivals** (Blizzard, 1990) and **Thirteen Hands** (1993). She is the winner of two National Magazine Awards (1984, 1985), a CBC Drama Award for the play **Women Waiting** (1983), second prize in the 1984 CBC short fiction competition, and the Marion Engel Award in 1990.

Carol Shields' 1993 novel **The Stone Diaries** (Random House) was nominated for the Booker Prize and won the Governor General's Award for Fiction.

Festival 10 (1992)

MEG'S PASTA DISH

My Toronto daughter, Meg, and her husband, Richard, whipped this up for me one night in ten minutes flat.

2 **cloves garlic,** minced
olive oil
1 medium jar **artichoke hearts in oil**
1/2 cup **black olives,** pitted and halved
2 **tomatoes,** seeded and chopped
2 tbsp **pine nuts** (optional)
handful chopped parsley or

chopped green onion or
fresh basil in ascending order of preference
1/4 cup **parmesan cheese**
 (they grind their own, but I don't)
1/2 lb **pasta, any sort**
salt and pepper

- Cook pasta, drain, rinse and drain again, toss with a little of the oil from artichokes. Keep warm.
- Saute garlic in oil, add other ingredients (using only a very little of the oil from artichokes). Stir into pasta and serve with extra cheese.

MY MOTHER'S LEMON DESSERT

My mother used to say that if you put good things in a dish, it would *turn out good!*

4 tbsp **butter**
1/2 cup **white sugar**
2 **eggs separated**

1 cup **milk**
2 tbsp **flour**
juice and rind of 1 lemon

- Cream butter and sugar. (This doesn't mean adding cream, which is what I did when I was a young bride.)
- Add egg yolks beaten until thick, stir in flour and milk, lemon juice and grated rind.
- Beat egg whites until stiff, and fold into mixture.
- Bake 25 minutes in buttered baking dish or custard cups set in pan of hot water. Moderate oven, 350˚F degrees. Serve hot, warm, cool or cold—however you like it.

If you double this recipe and call it a Lemon Souffle (which indeed it is), it is quite polite enough to round off a dinner party. Or to serve to the Queen for that matter.

JEFFREY SIMPSON

Jeffrey Simpson has won all three of Canada's highest literary prizes: the Governor General's Award for non-fiction writing, the National Magazine Award for political writing, and the National Newspaper Award for column writing.

Born in New York, Jeffrey Simpson moved to Canada at the age of ten; he was educated at Queen's University and the London School of Economics.

In 1972 he began a year's parliamentary internship in Ottawa, and the following year joined the *Globe & Mail*, writing for that newspaper from Toronto, Quebec and Ottawa, and between 1981 and 1984 from London, England, as European Bureau Chief. He has been the *Globe and Mail*'s national political columnist based in Ottawa since 1984. He appears frequently on both French and English television and radio. For many years he was a political panelist on CBC's newscast, *Sunday Report* and CBC Radio's *Morningside*. He has been a speaker at major conferences in Canada and abroad, and has been a fellow at the University of Alberta, the University of British Columbia and Queen's University. He spent ten months in 1993-94 as a John S. Knight Fellow at Stanford University.

His books include **The Discipline of Power** (1980), which won the Governor General's Award for non-fiction, and the bestselling **The Spoils of Power/The Politics of Patronage** (Harper Collins 1988). In his provocative study, **Faultlines: Struggling for a Canadian Vision** (HarperCollins, 1993), Jeffrey Simpson analyzes eight key issues in the Canadian national debate and identifies the behind-the-scenes power brokers who are shaping these issues and the new and fractious political order in our country.

Festival 10 (1992)

CHEESE AND NOODLE PIE

This is a recipe from my mother-in-law, since I hate cooking—but I love eating.

3/4 cup **all-purpose flour**
1/2 tsp **salt**
1/4 tsp **dry mustard**
2 cups **grated cheddar cheese**
1/4 cup **melted margarine**
2 cups **mild onions,** thinly sliced
2 tbsp **margerine**
1 cup **1/2 inch wide noodles,** cooked and drained

2 **eggs**
1 cup **milk,** heated
1/2 tsp **salt**
pepper
thyme
bacon bits or chopped ham (optional)
chopped spinach (optional)

- Mix flour, salt, dry mustard, 1 cup of the grated cheddar cheese and 1/4 cup melted margerine thoroughly in a bowl.
- Press evenly over bottom and sides of a deep 9" pie plate.
- Saute onions in 2 tablespoons of margerine until transparent. Combine with noodles. Spread this mixture in cheese crust. You can also add bits of ham, bacon or chopped spinach at this time.
- Beat eggs. Add milk, salt, pepper, thyme and the other cup of cheddar cheese.
- Bake at 325°F for 40 minutes or until crust is set. A little more cheese sprinkled on top a few minutes before removing from the oven is nice.
- This recipe is easily doubled or tripled—you'll need it.

ROBIN SKELTON

Born in Yorkshire in 1925, educated at Cambridge and Leeds universities, Robin Skelton taught at the University of Manchester for 12 years before coming to Canada in 1963 to teach at the University of Victoria. He was responsible for creating the special collections division of UVic's library and founded the university's creative writing Department.

He is the author or compiler of over 85 books and more than 30 chapbooks and broadsides of poetry, fiction, drama, history, biography, literary criticism, art criticism, verse translation and the occult. His poetry collections include **Collected Shorter Poems, 1947-1977**, and **Collected Longer Poems 1947-1977** (Sono Nis, 1981); **Wordsong: Twelve Ballads** (Sono Nis 1983); and **Popping Fuchsias** (Cacanadadada, 1992). His works of fiction include his short story collections **The Parrot Who Could** (Sono Nis, 1987) which was a runner-up for the Stephen Leacock Award; **Telling the Tale** (Porcupine's Quill, 1987); **Hanky Panky** (Sono Nis, 1990); and **Higgledy Piggledy** (Pulp Press, 1992). His long fiction includes the speculative novel **Fires of the Kindred** (Porcepic Books, 1987).

The Memoirs of a Literary Blockhead (Reference West, 1988) is an autobiograph-ical work, as is **Portrait of My Father** (Sono Nis, 1989), a 65-year-old son's charming biographical sketch of the father he resembles in many ways.

One of Canada's best-known male witches, Robin Skelton was called as an expert witness at Victoria's highly publicized 100 Huntley Street witchcraft trial which resulted in a legal distinction being made between Satanism and witchcraft. Among his books on witchcraft are **Spellcraft: A Handbook of Invocations and Blessings** (Sono Nis, 1978); **A Gathering of Ghosts** (Western Producer Prairie Books, 1989), the casebook of hauntings and attempted exorcisms that he undertook with Jean Kozocari; and **The Practice of Witchcraft** (Porcepic, 1990), a look at the myths, rituals, spells and terminology of modern witchcraft.

A fellow of the Royal Society of Literature and an ex-Chairman of the Writers' Union of Canada, Robin Skelton is the co-founder of *The Malahat Review* and served as its editor until 1982. At different periods of his life he has been a regular reviewer/columnist for the Manchester *Guardian*, the Victoria *Daily Times*, the Victoria *Times Colonist* and the Toronto *Star*.

Festival 9 (1991)

I only cook when forced to do so by circumstances beyond my control such as an absent or sick wife, and when I do cook my recipes are extremely unremarkable, though a curry I once made with chili powder lingers in the family memory, and I have been known to wield a mean wok.

Here therefore are two recipes that are certainly favorites of mine, but hardly haut cuisine. I do not comment on them. They neither require nor deserve comment.

POTAGE DE JOUR

- First select the appropriate can. Holding it in the left hand, read the instructions. Rotate it gently clockwise and read the instructions in English.
- Place the can on the kitchen counter and, holding it firmly with one hand, deploy a can opener with the other, rotating the can as the metal is sheared. Still holding the can firmly lift up the separated can top with your finger and thumb.
- Select an appropriately sized piece of Elastoplast from the first aid cupboard.
- Re-read the instructions on the can. Rotate the can and re-read the instructions in English.
- Pour the contents of the can into a saucepan. Fill the empty can with water or milk, as desired and as instructed, and empty the can into the saucepan. Make use of a paper towel.
- Place the pan on a hot plate and switch on the electrical power. Move the pan to another and glowing hot plate.
- Take a wooden spoon and stir the contents of the pan. Wait and observe. When small bubbles appear on the surface of the liquid, remove the pan from the hot plate and pour the contents into a bowl of the required shape and size. Make use of a paper towel. Serve.

CELERI ECOSSAIS

- First select previously cleaned celery sticks. Place them in a small tumbler.
- Now select a second glass of one cup capacity. Place ice cubes in the glass until they almost reach the rim of the glass. The cubes should be moderate size. No shaved ice should be included.
- Take a bottle of scotch whisky and fill the glass almost to the brim. Leave to mature for three minutes, then serve. Replace the celery in the refrigerator for later use.

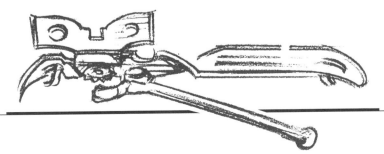

ELAINE STEVENS

Herbalist and writer Elaine Stevens is a co-author of one of the most popular west coast gardening books ever published, **The Twelve Month Gardener: A West Coast Guide** (Whitecap Books, 1991). Now in its fourth printing, the book continues to receive rave reviews from novice and expert gardeners alike for its practical, straightforward approach to west coast gardening. It leads gardeners month by month through the year, with lots of great tips and plant lists, and includes an invaluable resource section containing information on everything from specialty nurseries to composting supplies.

Elaine and her co-authors, Dagmar Hungerford, Doris Fancourt-Smith, Jane Mitchell and Ann Buffam, are all enthusiastic west coast gardeners who were frustrated by the lack of an up-to-date gardening guide for their area. "We were having to rely on books produced by gardeners living in other parts of North America, or in England, where conditions are vastly different from our own," they said. " We decided to see what we could pull together, and the final result surprised and delighted even us."

Since then the authors have produced a companion volume, **The Twelve Month Gardener's Journal** (Whitecap Books, 1992) and are all busy with their various gardening activities. This includes putting in as many volunteer hours as they can to assist with programs at Vancouver's two great botanical gardens, the Van Dusen Gardens and the University of B.C. Gardens. Dagmar is also well know to B.C. gardeners for her weekly Saturday morning spot on CBC radio, and she and Elaine are currently working on a new book. All we could find out is that "it will be published in the Spring of 1995, and will be an inspirational, fun book for gardeners, whether they live in Victoria, Moose Jaw, or the Gaspe Peninsula".

Besides writing and tending her garden, Elaine runs a busy clinical herbal practice and teaches herbal students and continuing education courses at the Wild Rose College of Natural Healing in Vancouver. She believes we all need to take more time to learn from plants, and use our gardens for spiritual and emotional nourishment as well as for physical health and healing.

Festival 10 (1992)

I inflict these two recipes on friends and family all the time and they seem to like them. Unfortunately, I'm not one of those cooks who measure—both the soup and the salad have evolved with me, and both depend upon what I have to hand, so they are always slightly different. The quantities I've given should work though, and people can do their own experimenting from there.

CARROT LEMON SOUP

1 **large onion, finely chopped**
2-3 tbsp **olive oil**
1 lb **carrots,** peeled and cut into 1/2" rounds
1 large **yam** or 1 small **squash**
  (winter, butternut or acorn)
  peeled and cut into 1/2" pieces.

1 pint **chicken stock**
Juice of 3 lemons
1/2 inch **fresh ginger root,** grated
2 tsp **ground cumin**
additional water if necessary

- Saute the onion in the olive oil in a covered pot until transparent. Add the other vegetables and continue to cook, covered, until they begin to soften.
- Add the chicken stock, ginger root and cumin. Cook until the vegetables are tender. Leave the soup to cool.
- Blend in a food processor until the soup is a fine puree.
- Add the lemon juice, and more water if necessary, to bring the soup to the correct consistency. Adjust the seasoning to taste with more lemon juice, cumin, and/or salt and pepper.
- Warm through to serve, sprinkled with a little parsley.

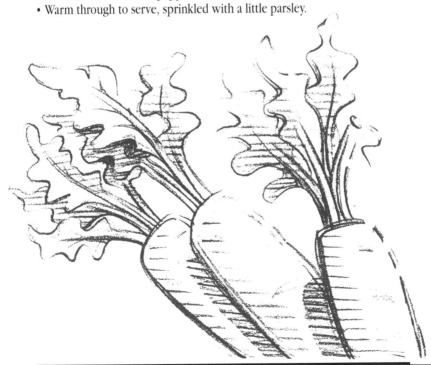

SHAKESPEARIAN SALAD

The challenge here is to make a salad without any lettuce, cucumber, tomato or other ingredients usually associated with contemporary salads. Instead, a Shakespearian salad uses a combination of wild and garden greens, herbs and flowers. It is an excellent starter for a meal in spring and summer when wild greens invade the garden and are young, tender and full of vitamins and minerals. Many of the wild greens are slightly bitter, making them an excellent tonic for the digestive system. For maximum benefit to health, eat the salad 15 to 20 minutes before the rest of the meal.

Any or all of the following can be put into the salad:

Wild greens such as **dandelion leaves, chickweed, miner's lettuce, lamb's quarters, young plantain leaves;**

Garden salad ingredients such as **sorrel, salad burnet, arugula, kale, parsley, sweet violet leaves, nasturtium leaves:**

Herbs such as **thyme, rosemary, oregano, marjoram, savory, mints.**

Flowers such as **sweet violets, primroses, nasturtiums, borage, rose petals, pot marigolds;**

- Wash and dry leaves and flowers. Mix leaves and herbs in bowl and toss with dressing (below). Decorate with the flowers and serve.

SALAD DRESSING:

1/2 tsp **Dijon mustard**
1 fl oz **apple cider vinegar or freshly squeezed lemon juice**

3 fl oz **extra virgin olive oil**
1 clove **garlic, crushed**
salt and pepper to taste

- Mix the mustard with the vinegar or lemon juice and the crushed garlic. Add the olive oil and mix well. Add salt and pepper to taste.
- Use enough of the dressing, as needed, to dress the salad lightly.

HILARY STEWART

Hilary Stewart, who lives on Quadra Island, B.C., is an award winning and critically acclaimed writer, artist, lecturer and consultant on Northwest Coast First Nations cultures. Born in the West Indies, she was educated mainly in England, including 4 years at St. Martin's School of Art in London, before coming to Canada in 1951.

By 1972 her continuing active interest in archaeology led her to abandon a 12-year career as Art Director of BCTV to research, write and illustrate **Artifacts of the Northwest Coast Indians** (Hancock 1973). As a result she was invited to photograph and illustrate **Images: Stone: BC**, written by anthropologist Wilson Duff (Hancock 1975), a catalogue of a travelling exhibition of 3,000 years of stone sculpture of this coast.

Expanding her field of interest in native cultures, Hilary Stewart researched, wrote and illustrated **Indian Fishing: Early Methods on the Northwest Coast** (J.J. Douglas 1977), and **Cedar: Tree of Life to the Northwest Coast Indians** (Douglas & McIntyre 1984). Both of these required gathering raw materials, learning technologies and making and using tools and implements for her research. Drawn to coastal First Nations art, she wrote **Robert Davidson: Haida Printmaker**, published in full colour, and followed it with **Looking at Indian Art of the Northwest Coast** (both D&M 1979). The latter has sold well over 100,000 copies. Two other art books are **Totem Poles** (D&M 1990) and a revised paperback version **Looking at Totem Poles** (D&M 1993), a guide to the history of 110 outdoor poles, defining the figures carved on them, the associated legends and how the poles were carved and raised. Illustrations are the writer's own detailed drawings.

Other books by Hilary Stewart, both richly illustrated, are **Wild Teas, Coffees and Cordials** (D&M 1981), and the extraordinary true story, **The Adventures and Sufferings of John R. Jewitt, Captive of Maquinna** (D&M 1987). **Cedar** and **John R. Jewitt** won B.C. Book Prizes awards, while **Robert Davidson** won the Pacific Northwest Booksellers Award (Seattle).

Hilary Stewart wrote the interpretive labelling for a major permanant exhibition of Indian and Eskimo cultures at Chicago's Field Museum. She has also guest curated three Canadian museum exhibits on the subjects of her books. She lectures extensively and is often the resource person on educational cruises and field trips. She is currently illustrating a book by anthropologist Joy Inglis on the petroglyphs of Quadra Island.

Festival 4 (1986)

Because I would much rather spend my time at my typewriter or drawing board than in the kitchen, having friends for dinner means nothing can be time consuming. These two desserts are quick and simple, but more important, they are delicious.

PRUNES-IN-PORT

1 package **soft prunes,** stoned	2 tbsp **sugar**
1 **orange**	1 cup **port**
4 cups **water**	

- Place prunes in a bowl, add zest and juice of orange.
- Add water, stir, let stand for 2 hours.
- Pour into saucepan, add sugar, and simmer very gently for 1 hour.
- Pour into serving bowl, and while still hot add port.
- Allow to cool, chill, and serve with ice cream, frozen yoghourt or cream.

PEAR DELIGHT

This one is so simple it only has two ingredients and cooks itself while you are having dinner.

2 cans **Bartlett pears**
1 box **After Eight chocolate mints**

- Place pear halves, flat side down, in a casserole dish or baking pan, adding liquid from can.
- Top each pear with an After Eight mint.
- Cook in a very slow oven 225°F for about an hour.
- The chocolate melts in dribbles over the pear and the minty flavour is intriguing.

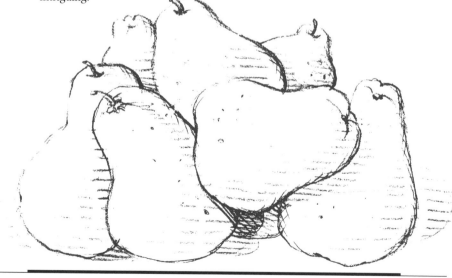

ROBERT B. *T*URNER

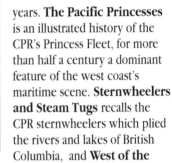

Robert Turner never planned to work in the museum field. With a BA in Geography from the University of Victoria and an MA in Regional Planning from UBC, he had gone to work for the Provincial Parks Branch, but transferred to B.C.'s Provincial Museum in 1973 when they advertised for another curator in the Modern History Division to prepare exhibits for the Museum Train which began operating in 1974. He stayed on after the train stopped running in 1979, and in time became chief of historical collections at the museum.

His first book, **Vancouver Island Railroads**, grew out of his frustration at finding that virtually nothing had been published on B.C.'s transportation and industrial history. Curiosity prompted the writing of **Railroaders, Recollection from the Steam Era of British Columbia** and **The Princess Marguerite. Logging By Rail: The British Columbia Story** (Sono Nis, 1990) documents the dramatic story of the logging railroad era in B.C.

Robert Turner has written four books, all published by Sono Nis, detailing the role of the Canadian Pacific Railway and Steamship Companies in this province. **The Pacific Empresses** recounts the history of CP's trans-Pacific liners that dominated passenger service on the North Pacific for over 50 years. **The Pacific Princesses** is an illustrated history of the CPR's Princess Fleet, for more than half a century a dominant feature of the west coast's maritime scene. **Sternwheelers and Steam Tugs** recalls the CPR sternwheelers which plied the rivers and lakes of British Columbia, and **West of the Great Divide** is the history of the Canadian Pacific Railway in British Columbia.

Robert Turner worked as a consultant to the Canadian Parks Service on the preservation of the historic sternwheeler *Moyie*, beached at Kaslo on Kootenay Lake. His book, **The S.S. Moyie: Memories of the Oldest Sternwheeler** (Sono Nis) relates the role played by the pioneer ship from 1898 to her retirement in 1957.

After nearly 20 years with B.C.'s Provincial Museum, Robert Turner returned to university to do research and to spend more time writing. He now holds the honourary position of Curator Emeritus at the museum where he will do some volunteer projects in the next few years. His next book, co-authored with Dave Wilkie, will be on the Kaslo & Slocan Railway, a narrow gauge line built in 1895 to bring out ore from the mines of Sandon and the Slocan in B.C.'s Kootenay district.

Festival 2 (1984)

CANADIAN PACIFIC CHRISTMAS PUDDING

This recipe has become a Christmas tradition for our family. Each fall we make a batch of puddings, often along with friends, and then freeze them for Christmas. We have also sent puddings along to friends, particularly those with an interest in shipping or railroad travel. Wrapped in aluminum foil and tied in a plastic bag and well packed, they ship well and we have had no reports of any being spoiled in transit. This is a rich pudding and a small serving is usually plenty.

In both recipes, the festiveness of the cooking is usually improved if at least an equal amount of the brandy is provided to each participant in the cooking as is administered to the Christmas pud or the sauce. Wine may be substituted for serving to the cooks.

These recipes were given to me by Deborah Hertzberg and the recipes have direct connections to the Canadian Pacific Steamships. I included them in my book **The Pacific Empresses**. I am collecting more for inclusion in a book in preparation on the CPR's North Atlantic steamships as well as ones from the railway services across Canada.

rind of 1 lemon	1 cup **cherries** 250 ml
1/4 lb **candied lemon peel** 125 g	5 **eggs,** beaten
1/8 lb **candied citron peel** 65 g	1/2 cup **flour** 125 ml
1 lb **raisins** 500 g	1/2 tbsp **ginger** 10 ml
1/2 lb **currants** 250 g	3/4 tsp **cinnamon** 4 ml
1/2 lb **brown sugar** 250 g	1/4 oz **allspice** 8 g
1/4 lb **bread crumbs** 125 g	half **nutmeg,** grated
1 **carrot,** grated	**1 wineglass brandy or port**
1/2 lb **suet, ground** 250 g	(or to taste—1 cup or 250 ml is fine).

- Mix the first ten ingredients together in a large bowl:
- In another bowl mix the next six ingredients thoroughly and add them to the first first bowl of ingredients and mix well together.
- Add brandy or port.
- Fill pudding bowls two-thirds full. Cover tightly and boil for at least four hours.
- To reheat boil again for two hours.
- (We substitute butter for the ground suet to produce a lighter pudding, one which is also preferable for vegetarians).
- Toppings can be varied to taste. Whipped cream or ice cream are excellent but more traditional would be a hard sauce. A brandy sauce recipe follows.

CANADIAN PACIFIC BRANDY SAUCE

2 tbsp **butter** 30 ml
1/3 cup **sugar** 75 ml
1/2 cup **boiling water** 125 ml
2 tsp **cornstarch** 10 ml

1/2 cup **milk** 125 ml
2 **egg yolks**
2-4 tbsp **brandy** 30-60 ml

- Melt butter in a saucepan, add sugar and boiling water.
- Dissolve cornstarch with 2 tbsp of the milk.
- Beat egg yolks with a fork, then beat the remainder of the milk with them.
- Add the dissolved cornstarch.
- Stir constantly until the sauce thickens—about 10 minutes.
- Remove from heat and stir in the brandy.

BETTY WATERTON

A seventh generation Canadian, Betty Waterton was born in Oshawa, Ontario. In 1934 the family moved to Vancouver, where Betty soon began writing reams of rhyming poems. Some of these were kindly published in the local press. In 1942 she married an R.C.A.F. pilot, and after the war, while raising three children, she studied art, worked briefly as a retoucher at the Vancouver *Sun*, did television animation and painted portraits.

When her children were grown, Betty Waterton began writing children's books. Her first book, **A Salmon for Simon**, was published by Douglas & McIntyre in 1978. It was runner-up for the Canadian Library Association's Book of the Year for Children Award and a co-winner of the Canada Council Children's Literature Prize. In 1984 the same book made the Children's Choice Award list of the Washington Library Media Association. **Pettranella** (Douglas & McIntyre, 1980) was a finalist for the Canadian Library Association Book of the Year for Children Award.

In 1984 Betty Waterton published the first in her seven-book series of Quincy Rumpel stories. **Quincy Rumpel** (1984), **Starring Quincy Rumpel** (1986), **Quincy Rumpel, P.I.** (1988), **Morris Rumpel and the Wings of Icarus** (1989), **Quincy Rumpel and the Sasquatch of Phantom Cove** (1991), **Quincy Rumpel and the Woolly Chaps** (1992), and **Quincy Rumpel and the Mystifying Experience** (1994)—all published under the Douglas & McIntyre/Groundwood imprint—They feature the 12-year old Quincy and her scatter-brained family.

Betty Waterton's other children's books are **Mustard** (Scholastic, 1983 and 1992), **The White Moose** (Ginn, 1984), and **Plain Noodles** (Groundwood, 1989). Her books have been published internationally.
Festival 7 (1989)

QUINCY RUMPEL'S TOMATO SOUP

- Heat gently and separately 1 can of tomatoes and an equal quantity of milk (canned, whole or skim). Do not bring either to the boiling point.
- Add a bit of baking soda to the tomatoes and stir.
- When heated, add some butter, pepper and salt and cracker crumbs to the tomatoes.
- Add the hot milk, being careful not to let the mixture boil. Serve immediately.

DREAM CAKE

1 3/4 cups **flour**
1/2 cup **brown sugar**
3/4 cup **butter or margerine**
1 or 2 **eggs**
1 cup **brown sugar**

1/2 tsp **baking powder**
1 cup **chopped nuts**
1 cup **raisins**
chopped preserved ginger (optional)

- Mix flour, brown sugar and butter or margarine as shortbread and press into shallow greased pan (9" x 9" or thereabouts).
- Mix the remaining ingredients.
- Spread on top of shortbread mixture and bake very slowly. Cut while hot.

BEN WICKS

Cartoonist, author and television host Ben Wicks was born a block from London Bridge. He left school at age fourteen, and worked as a fruit seller, clog maker, wallet maker, army shipping clerk and musician.

After his immigration to Canada in 1957, he developed a career as a newspaper cartoonist. Now distributed by South News Syndicate, he is one of the most widely distributed political cartoonists in the world. His books of cartoons include **Ben Wicks' Canada, Ben Wicks' Women, Ben Wicks' Book of Losers, Ben Wicks' Book of Etiquette, More Losers, Ben Wicks' Dogs, So You Want to Be Prime Minister, The First** (and **Second**) **Treasury of Ben Wicks**, and **Ben Wicks and Company**.

In 1987 Ben Wicks published his first book about World War II and the devastating effect it had on the people who were left behind when the boys went off to battle. **No Time To Wave Goodbye** (Stoddart), which spent 10 weeks on the London *Sunday Times* best seller list and 16 weeks on the Canadian best seller list, is the collected reminiscences of British child evacuees. It was followed in 1989 by a second book of reminiscences, **The Day They Took the Children** (Stoddart) which was on the London *Sunday Times* best seller list for 8 weeks, reaching number 6. **Nell's War** (Stoddart, 1990), published in England as **Waiting for the All Clear**, looked at the war as his mother had experienced it in London. Next in the series came **When The Boys Came Marching Home** (Stoddart, 1991) and then **Promise You'll Take Care of My Daughter** (Stoddart, 1992), the story of British war brides in Canada.

Ben Wicks covered the Biafran War for the Los Angeles *Times* Syndicate and lived with the rebels of northern Ethiopia to report on Africa's longest war for the Toronto *Star*. *The World of Wicks*, which ran for 6 years on network television, involved travelling around the world to conduct on-the-spot interviews with some of the leading figures of our time. In 1986, he was presented with the Order of Canada.

Festival 9 (1991)

STEWING BEEF STEW

2 lbs **stewing beef**
2 tbsp **flour**
2 tbsp **oil**
1/4 cup **tomato sauce**
2 cups **boiling water**
1 tsp **salt**

1/2 tsp **pepper**
1/2 tsp **sugar**
6 **potatoes**
4 **carrots**
2 **medium onions**
1 cup **peas**

- Cook in a large saucepan on top of stove.
- Roll stewing beef in flour.
- Heat oil and add stewing beef.
- Cook until beef is slightly done.
- Add salt, pepper, sugar, tomato sauce and mix well.
- Pour boiling water over meat.
- Cover and simmer for one and a half hours.
- In a separate saucepan cook potatoes, carrots, onions and peas.
- About 20 minutes before beef is ready, add cooked vegetables.
- Serves four people

RICE PUDDING

1 1/2 cups **uncooked rice**
1/2 cup of **sugar**
2 cups **milk**
1 tbsp **butter**

- Place uncooked rice on the bottom of a loaf pan.
- Add sugar, milk and butter
- Cook at 325°F in oven for one and a half hours.
- Serves 4 people.

DANIEL WOOD

Daniel Wood has worked as a writer/editor/ broad-caster/photographer for eighteen years. He is the author of eleven books including the novel, **The River of Gold**; a Social Studies textbook, **Exploring Our Country**; and a children's book, **No Clothes**.

He has also written scores of magazine articles for such periodicals as *Saturday Night, Destinations, Maclean's, Geo, Chatelaine, Islands, Vancouver Magazine, Discovery, Equinox* and *Western Living*. As well, he has written more than 50 scripts for David Suzuki's science program *Discovery*, and has appeared on such CBC programs as *The Journal, Morningside*, and *The Early Edition*.

Prior to working as a writer, Daniel Wood taught in the Faculty of Education at UBC. During that time he wrote **Kids! Kids! Kids!**, one of the most successful books in Canadian publishing history with over 135,000 copies sold.

Daniel Wood has travelled extensively, visiting almost half the world's countries and living in Denmark, Nepal, Malaysia, and Greece. His recent writing and photographic assignments have placed him in a variety of unusual situations. He has been treed by a pair of unhappy rhinos in southern Nepal, spent a week in Africa's Kalahari Desert with the last nomadic Bushmen, wandered amid the gunfire of Nicaragua's civil war, and gotten drunk on *tuak* with Borneo's Iban tribesmen. In his travels he has eaten, among other things, giraffe, porcupine, civet cat, puff adder, whale, crocodile, elephant, guinea pig, monkey, iguana, and a number of other creatures of uncertain identity.

In the 1980s, he served on the national executive of the Periodical Writers Association of Canada, as president of B.C. Writers Federation, and as president of the Western Magazine Awards. He has taught writing during the last decade at UBC and Simon Fraser University.

Daniel Wood has received six finalist nominations and won the Gold Award in the National Magazine Awards. As well, he has been nominated twenty-four times as a finalist in the Western Magazine Awards, winning eight times. He is considered one of Canada's leading magazine writers.

Workshops Summer 1986, Summer 1991, Fall 1991 and Summer 1992

HOW TO BAKE A SNAKE

"DOWN UNDER" takes on a new meaning in this Australian recipe. First you have to get the snake DOWN, and if you don't cook it right, you could be UNDER forever.

- If a snake is killed and thrown straight on to the fire, it immediately twists and turns into a very disconcerting shape indeed.
- To cook it properly, you need a fire and two people. They sit one each side of the fire and stretch the snake over the heat, passing it to and fro slowly, to keep it straight.

VEAL MEATBALLS IN SPICY CHORIZO SAUCE

I like tapas-style potluck suppers with friends because it's all little delectable morsels, flavorful and sociable food perfect for nibbling.

Bar Casa Ruperto, in the Triana section of Sevilla across the Guadalquivir River, is an unprepossessing bar, yet its tapas are quite extraordinary. Owner Ruperto Blanco has devised an intriguing sauce ("All our cooking here is pure artisanship!") that includes chorizo, blood sausage, coriander, and cumin. He serves it with snails, but also uses similar ingredients as a marinade for pork and quail. I have used the sauce here to flavor meatballs, and it also works exceptionally well with scallops.

THE SAUCE:

1 tbsp **olive oil**
1 small **chorizo sausage (2 oz)**, skinned and minced
2 cloves **garlic**, minced
1 small **tomato**, skinned and chopped
2 **pimiento**, chopped

1 tsp **coriander seed**, crushed
1/2 tsp **cumin seed**, freshly crushed
1/4 tsp **paprika, preferably Spanish style**
1/2 **dried red chili pepper**, crumbled OR
1/4 tsp **crushed red pepper**
2 tbsp **chicken broth**

THE MEATBALLS:

1 lb **ground veal**
4 tbsp **dry white wine**
2 **eggs**, lightly beaten
5 tbsp **bread crumbs**
2 stalks **celery**, finely minced
1 onion, finely minced
1 clove **garlic**, minced

1 tbsp **cilantro**, minced
dash **salt, freshly ground pepper, paprika, marjoram, basil, celery seed, chives, onion powder, worcestershire sauce**
4 tbsp **olive oil**

(Continued on pg. 138)

To make the sauce:
- Heat the oil and saute the chorizo slowly for a minute or two. Stir in the garlic, then add the tomato, pimento, coriander, cumin, paprika, and chili pepper.
- Cover and simmer for 5 minutes.
- Transfer to a processor and blend until as smooth as possible. With the motor running, thin gradually with 2 tablespoons or more of chicken broth to a sauce consistency.

To make the meatballs:
- Combine the veal with 1 tablespoon of white wine, eggs, bread crumbs, celery, onion, garlic, cilantro, salt and pepper and all other spices.
- Form into small balls (about 1 1/4 inches). Heat the oil in a skillet and brown the meatballs well on all sides.
- Add the prepared sauce, the remaining 3 tablespoons of wine, and the chicken broth. Cover and simmer for 20 minutes.

Serves 6
Double the recipe for good leftovers.

CAROLINE WOODWARD

Caroline Woodward, who lives in B.C.'s Slocan Valley, has been writing and publishing fiction, book reviews, scripts, and letters to politicians since 1968. **Disturbing the Peace** (Polestar: 1990), her first collection of short fiction, was nominated for the Ethel Wilson Fiction Prize in 1991. Stories from this collection have since appeared in high school texts and have been included on university level contemporary Canadian literature and writing courses.

Her mystery novel, **Alaska Highway Two-Step**, was published by Polestar in May 1993. Margaret Cannon of the *Globe and Mail* in reviewing this novel wrote "Woodward has a marvelous eye for setting and detail . . . . She also shows a talent for research and a flair for character development." Recently she collaborated with a musical clown and trapeze artist on a two-act stage play **Where's the Net?**

Her non-fiction work has been published in *Conservation Canada*, *Books in Canada*, the *Globe & Mail*, *Quill & Quire*, *Images*, the *Kootenay Review*, *Event* and *Descant*. Her poetry and fiction have appeared in such prestigious journals as *Prism International*, *The Malahat Review*, *This Magazine*, *Canadian Fiction Magazine*, *Writing*, *Swiftcurrent*, *Images*, *Geist* and eight Canadian literary anthologies.

Caroline Woodward has been an organizer and instructor with the Kootenay School of Writing, the Kootenay School of the Arts and the Summer School of the Arts in Nelson. She has also taught for Selkirk College, and served on the boards of Theatre Energy and the Federation of B.C. Writers, and is currently on the board of Selkirk College. She has served on juries for the Canada Council and the B.C./Yukon National Book Festival Program.

She is the co-owner and operator of the Motherlode Bookstore in New Denver, B.C.
Festival 10 (1992) & Workshops Summer 1990 and Fall 1991

MOUNTAIN BLUEBERRY PANCAKES

One of our favourite Sunday morning breakfasts, at home or in the bush, is Mountain Blueberry Pancakes. Saskatoons, wild raspberries or small chunks of apple also taste great, in pre- and post- blueberry season.

3 cups **flour**
6 tsp **baking powder**
3 tbsp **brown sugar**
1 tsp **salt**
1 **egg, beaten** (or 1 tbsp arrowroot powder plus 2 tbsp H2O)
1 1/2 cups **milk** (for a very thick batter or 2 - 2 1/2 cups for runnier mix)
1/4 cup **melted butter**
1 tsp **vanilla**
1 cup **floured blueberries (or whatever)**

- Sift and stir the first four ingredients.
- Mix the egg, milk, melted butter and vanilla and add them to the dry ingredients.
- Fold in 1 cup of floured blueberries.
- Fry on hot griddle.
- Use real maple syrup! On one camping trip, we made a fruit sauce instead of syrup, using up the 4-day-old, bottom-of-the-pack bruised fruit: plums, apricots, apples and a handful of wild blackberries plus a shot of real vanilla. This was 5☆!

VALHALLA'S BEST BANNOCK DINNER

The following recipe is the result of inventive camping cookery during the summer of 1992 in Valhalla Wilderness Park, near New Denver. We have tested, adapted and refined this recipe to our satisfaction. We trust you will be able to replicate a campfire (dry birch driftwood works nicely) wherever you are in Canada, to get that special outdoor taste. Bon appetit!

2 cups **whole-wheat flour**
2 tsp **baking powder**
pinch of salt
1/4 cup **non-instant dried milk**
1/2 tsp **dill weed or basil** (optional)
1/4 cup **parmesan or grated monterey jack tofurella cheese** (optional)

- Put all these ingredients into a yoghurt container or some other spill-proof camping container.
- Drive, canoe, kayak or hike to your favourite picnic spot.
- Add about 1 cup of water, 1/4 cup at a time and stir bannock mixture with a peeled stick or wooden spoon. Set aside, covered.
- Roast tofu wiener or the mystery meat ones, if you must, on sturdy pointed sticks until bubbly and hot.
- Tear off a chunk of bannock dough and wrap it around the wiener. Some of us make a foot-long rope of bannock and wind it around the hot wiener. (The hot wiener seems to speed the cooking process; while the fire is roasting the outside, the heat of the wiener helps to cook the bannock right next to it, avoiding the over-cooked outside and raw dough inside effect.) A fairly thin layer must be used for the wraparound but some bannock lovers like to encase the entire wiener in a one centimetre thick blanket.
- Return wiener to campfire and turn it slowly until the bannock has puffed out nicely to a dark golden brown colour. Several taste-testers recommend spreading Dijon mustard or other condiments on the hot wiener prior to wrapping it in bannock. Whatever you choose to do, the time it takes to perfect the wraparound bannock you like best makes this humble dinner as much fun to make as it is to eat.

L. R. (BUNNY) WRIGHT

Novelist Laurali Rose "Bunny" Wright graduated from high school in Soest, West Germany, and later attended the Universities of B.C. and Calgary, Carleton University and the Banff School of Fine Arts. Her career has included working as a copywriter for a California advertising agency, acting with Holiday Theatre (the children's theatre company that toured B.C. schools during the 1960s and '70s) and 8 years of reporting for the Calgary *Herald*. She is presently enrolled in an M.A. (Liberal Studies) program at Simon Fraser University.

Bunny Wright's first published novel, **Neighbours** (Macmillan, 1979) is the story of a suburban housewife being driven insane by loneliness; it won her the Search for a New Alberta Novelist Award. Next came **The Favourite** (Doubleday, 1982), and **Among Friends** (Doubleday, 1984), both of them Literary Guild selections. **Love In The Temperate Zone** (Viking Penguin in the U.S. and Macmillan in Canada) was published in 1988.

The Suspect (Viking Penguin/Doubleday, 1985) was the first of Bunny Wright's mystery stories. Featuring Staff Sergeant Alberg, it uncovers passion and murder among Sechelt's senior citizens, and it won her the Edgar Allan Poe Award for the best mystery novel of the year. Alberg's further adventures on the Sunshine Coast appeared in **Sleep While I Sing** (1986, Viking Penguin in the U.S. and Doubleday in Canada) and again in **Chill Rain In January** (Viking/Macmillan of Canada, 1990) which won the Crime Writers of Canada Arthur Ellis Award for Best Mystery Novel. **Fall From Grace**, published in 1991 by Seal Books in Canada and Viking Penguin in the U.S., was another Literary Guild selection. **Prized Possessions** (Doubleday) marked Staff Sergeant Alberg's fifth adventure in Sechelt's murder and mayhem department. The sixth book in the series, **A Touch of Panic**, will be published in 1994.

Bunny Wright's mystery stories have been published in the United Kingdom, Japan, Sweden, West Germany, Italy, Norway, Spain and France. She is a member of the Writers' Union of Canada, International P.E.N., The International Association of Crime Writers, The Mystery Writers of America and The Crime Writers of Canada.

Festival 5 (1987) & Workshop Spring 1991

ARTICHOKE SALAD

1 pint **cherry tomatoes**
2 - 14 oz cans **artichoke hearts,** well drained
14 oz can **hearts of palm,** well drained
1/2 tsp **black pepper,** freshly ground

1 - 2 tsp **ground cumin**
1/4 cup **red wine vinegar**
2/3 cup **olive oil**

- Cut cherry tomatoes in half. Cut artichoke hearts in half or quarters, depending on their size; scrape out all the "choke" from each heart. Cut hearts of palm in half lengthwise and then into 1 1/2 inch pieces.
- Combine vegetables. Sprinkle with pepper and 1 tsp. cumin. Combine vinegar and oil and add to vegetables. Toss ingredients together well.
- Refrigerate salad a few hours or even overnight to blend flavours. Taste before serving and add more cumin or some salt. (Hearts of palm are pretty salty; you might not need any more salt.)
- Makes eight servings.

LEMON PARFAIT

1/2 cup **fresh lemon juice**
1 tbsp **grated lemon rind**
3 large **eggs,** separated
1 cup **granulated sugar,** divided

pinch **cream of tartar**
1 cup **cold whipping cream**
3 tbsp **icing sugar**
slivered lemon rind for garnish

- In small, heavy stainless steel or enamel saucepan, combine lemon juice, grated rind, egg yolks and 1/2 cup granulated sugar; beat mixture until well combined.
- Cook over moderate heat, stirring constantly, until mixture thickens. Do not let mixture boil. Transfer to large bowl and let cool.
- In bowl, beat egg whites and cream of tartar until soft peaks form. Add remaining 1/2 cup granulated sugar, one tablespoon at a time, beating until stiff peaks form. Fold meringue into lemon mixture.
- Beat cream until soft peaks form. Beat in icing sugar, beating until stiff. Fold whipped cream into lemon mixture. Divide among eight one-cup stemmed glasses. Chill. Garnish with slivered lemon rind.
- Makes eight servings.

MAX WYMAN

Max Wyman emigrated to Canada from England in 1967. A man versed in all the arts, he served as dance, music and drama critic for the Vancouver *Sun* for the next 13 years, switching in 1981 to Vancouver's *Province* newspaper to become arts columnist and dance critic. From 1988 to 1990 he was also drama critic, and he took on the duties of books editor in 1989. He returned to the *Sun* in 1992 as editor of the *Saturday Review* magazine.

His dance and theatre commentaries and reviews have been heard regularly on national CBC programming since 1975, and he has contributed frequently to publications ranging from *Maclean's* and *Performing Arts in Canada* to *The New York Times* and New York's *Dance-Magazine*, and a variety of international encyclopedias and anthologies.

He is the author of **The Royal Winnipeg Ballet: the First Forty Years** (Doubleday, 1978). His lavishly illustrated chronicle of Canadian dance, **Dance Canada: An Illustrated History** (Douglas & McIntyre, 1989), describes the growth of both ballet and modern dance in Canada from colonial times to the present. **Evelyn Hart: An Intimate Biography** (McClelland & Stewart 1991)is a revelation of the very private person beneath the professional stage persona of this star of the ballet world.

Max Wyman also edited **Vancouver Forum I** (Douglas & McIntyre, 1993), the first of a planned series of collections of provocative writings giving voice to the forces that are transforming the city of Vancouver. He is presently at work preparing **Vancouver Forum II**, and writing his "massive biography" of Oleg Vinogradov, artistic director of the Kirov Ballet in St. Petersburg.

He has served on many national arts juries and served two terms as a member of the Canada Council's dance advisory panel. Among his awards is the Queen's Jubilee medal and the 1991 B.C. Newspaper Award for feature-writing for a 14-part series on life in Russia.

Festival 9 (1991)

OLD-FASHIONED CHRISTMAS CAKE

This Christmas cake is one that I ran in The *Province* (when I was working there) a couple of times: readers kept writing in asking for it again because they'd lost the original. I make it every year; it's one of those ceremonial winter-afternoon celebration rituals. Make it well ahead of the season and let it mature (feeding it the while).

8 oz **butter**
8 oz **brown sugar**
grated rind of 1 lemon
5 **eggs**
10 oz **flour**
1 tbsp **liquid honey**
5 oz **chopped candied peel,**
   glace cherries, etc.
1/2 tsp **vanilla essence**

1/2 tsp **ground cinnamon**
1/2 tsp **ground mixed spices**
1/2 tsp **baking powder**
1/4 tsp **salt**
12 oz **currants**
12 oz **light raisins**
sherry or rum (your choice:
   both work wonderfully)

- Measure everything out first.
- In a large bowl, soften and beat the butter; add the sugar, and beat them together until they are creamy. Add the lemon rind. Beat in the eggs, one at a time, adding a little sifted flour after each. Stir in the honey.
- Mix the remaining flour, cinnamon, dry spices, baking powder and salt in a separate bowl, then stir this mixture into the main bowl in three stages—following each addition with one-third of the candied fruit, currants and raisins. It will thicken up quite satisfyingly; anyone who wants to help stir should be encouraged to do so. Stir in the vanilla at the end, then the sherry or rum; a couple of tablespoons or so will probable do the trick—what you want is a fairly dense batter that makes a thick splat in the bowl when you shake the spoon. Have a glass yourself.
- Pre-heat the oven to 325°F. Line a 9-inch cake tin with three or four layers of wax paper. Put the batter in the tin and let it settle to the sides. Place tin in the middle of the oven. Reduce the temperature to 285°F after 15 minutes, and start checking the cake after three hours. What you want is a rich brown colour; when it's done it should have shrunk slightly from the sides of the tin. Test its doneness with a warm metal or wood skewer at the centre; if it comes out clean, the cake's done. If you're happy with the colour and it still needs some baking time, cover the top with more wax paper until cooking's finished.
- Store it in a cake tin until eating time, wrapped in its original wax papers and a layer of tinfoil. Feed it every week or so with sherry or rum. Have a glass yourself.

WEST COAST COULIBIAKA

This is a version of a great Russian dish specially adapted to take advantage of one of B.C.'s great natural resource, the salmon. It is not necessarily a winter dish, but in our house it usually is. Traditionally, it's made in a loaf pan, with everything contained in a neat package. I prefer to let it languish on a large cookie sheet: it comes out shallower and wider, with more golden brioche surface. Cut it in cross-slices for serving. I freeze the leftovers (if there are any, they freeze well) and surprise unexpected drop-ins.

Set some time aside for this one. First you have to make the brioche dough. People shy away from making brioche, but it's really easy. These are the ingredients:

1 package (tbsp) **dry yeast**	1/2 tsp **salt**
1/4 cup **lukewarm water**	2 tsp **sugar**
2 cups **all-purpose flour**	3 **large eggs (or 4 small ones)**
10 tbsp **butter**	

• Dissolve the yeast in the water. Add half a cup of flour and stir with a fork or a scraper into a firm ball. On a floured board, knead this ball until it's smooth. Put a deep X in the top with knife, then drop the ball into a little bowl of lukewarm water. Soften the butter and cream it in a bowl. In a mixer bowl, put the rest of flour (1 1/2 cups), the salt, sugar and eggs. Beat these ingredients together. Add butter and mix well. Add the yeast, which should by now be floating somewhere near the surface of its little bowl. Mix the whole thing thoroughly; it becomes quite elastic, and tends to stick to the mixer beaters in a gooey kind of way, but persevere. When you've got a nice, smoothish dough (little lumps of yeast are okay), put it into a large, lightly floured bowl, cover the top with plastic wrap and a towel, and let it rise at room temperature. When it has risen to about double size, break the rise (run your finger round the rim). Stick the whole thing in the freezer for at least two hours.

Meanwhile . . . the filling. Here are the ingredients:

2 pounds **B.C. salmon fillet, cooked, skinned and broken into chunks**	1 tsp **garlic, chopped**
	1 cup **sour cream**
2 - 3 tbsp **breadcrumbs**	4 **eggs, hard-boiled and chopped**
1/4 cup **butter, melted**	**pepper**
2 tbsp **fresh dill, chopped**	**lemon juice**
1 medium-to-large **onion, chopped**	1 **beaten egg**

- When you're ready, preheat the oven to 375°F and roll out half the brioche dough into a kind of oval. It doesn't need to be too tidy a shape. Transfer it (carefully) to a well-buttered cookie tray. Repair any tears that might have occurred by pressing them together. It's all going to be brioche anyway.
- Mix the breadcrumbs and the melted butter in a bowl, and add half the garlic, half the dill and all the onion. In another bowl, mix the sour cream, chopped eggs, the rest of the garlic and dill and some pepper. Spread about half of the breadcrumbs/onion mixture across the brioche dough on the cookie tray. Spread about half the sour cream/eggs mixture over that. Arrange the broken-up chunks of salmon on top of this, making sure there's an even spread around the brioche base; sprinkle them with lemon juice. On top of the salmon, spread the rest of the sour cream/eggs mixture. On top of that spread the rest of the breadcrumbs/onion mixture. Roll out the rest of the brioche dough, brush the outer edges of the lower layer with beaten egg, and place the new layer of brioche (carefully) over the whole thing, being sure to seal the edges where the two layers meet.
- Let your creation stand for 20 minutes under a cloth covering (being sure the cloth doesn't touch the dough—I usually make a kind of concave medieval tent from a tea-towel with its ends tucked under four tall glasses). Then brush the top with beaten egg and bake for 30 -40 minutes. You can tell when it's done; the brioche rises and goes a wonderful golden colour. Let it stand a few minutes.

This recipe will easily serve six; maybe you'll have some ends and corners left over. Serve it with simple vegetables: green beans sauteed with toasted almonds; steamed carrots sauteed with sliced preserved ginger; and a side sauce of horseradish mixed with sour cream.

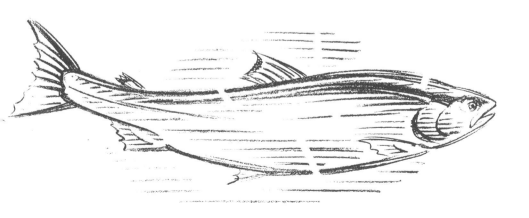

TIM WYNNE-JONES

Tim Wynne-Jones' series of children's books featuring the adventurous cat "Zoom" began with Zoom At Sea (Groundwood, 1983) which won the I.O.D.E. Toronto Chapter Award for Best Children's Book and the Canadian Booksellers' Ruth Schwartz Award). The cat's adventures continued in the Groundwood-published books Zoom Away (1985), and Zoom Upstream (1992). His other books for children are The Architect of the Moon (1988), Mischief City (1986), I'll Make You Small (1986), The Hour of the Frog (1989) and The Last Piece of Sky (1993), all published by Groundwood; and Mouse in a Manger (1993), published by Viking. His short story collection, Some of the Kinder Planets (Groundwood), won the 1993 Governor General's Award for children's Literature.

Tim Wynne-Jones is also the author of adult fiction. His first was the chilling mystery story, **Odd's End** (McClelland & Stewart), which won the 1980 Seal First Novel Award and was published in the U.S., Britain (where it was runner-up for the John Creasey Award) and Germany. It was followed by **The Knot** (McClelland & Stewart, 1983), which was the runner-up for the City of Toronto Book Award, and

Fastyngange (Lester & Orpen Dennys, 1988) which was retitled **Voices** for release in Britain, Spain and South America. All three novels were republished in paperback by McClelland & Stewart in 1990. His short stories have appeared in numerous anthologies.

Tim Wynne-Jones has written 3 radio dramas for CBC's *Nightfall*, a 3-part series (*Dust is the Only Secret*) for *Morningside* and five plays for *Vanishing Point*, including the musical **We Now Return You to Your Regularly Scheduled Universe** co-authored with Eric Rosser. He won an ACTRA award for his radio drama **St. Anthony's Man**. His music credits also include the book and lyrics for Toronto Young People's Theatre production of **Mischief City**, book and libretto for the Canadian Children's Opera Chorus production of a **Midwinter Night's Dream** and sixteen songs for the CBC/Jim Henson television show **Fraggle Rock**.

From 1985 to 1988 he was children's book reviewer for the Globe & Mail, and has been children's book editor for Red Deer College Press since 1989.

Festival 10 (1992)

EGGPLANT SZECHUAN

- Cut an eggplant in half, soak in cold water for 10 minutes, squeeze out water. Repeat 4 times.
- Cut eggplant in strips (skin on or off as desired).
- Start up Wok with oil, garlic diced small;
- Cook the eggplant until slightly brown.
- Add seasoning sauce.
- Stir until it thickens.
- Add shredded green onions.
- Stir and serve.

Seasoning Sauce:
Mix the following ingredients in a bowl:

2 tbsp **soy sauce**	1/2 tsp **honey**
1/2 tbsp **corn starch**	3 tbsp **water**
1/2 tbsp **sesame oil**	1 tbsp **hot bean paste** (or more!)

PASTA E FAGIOLI

1 1/4 cups **dried navy or peabeans**	1-2 cloves **garlic, crushed**
1 1/2 tsp **salt**	1 tsp **oregano** (or more)
2/3 cup **olive oil**	1 tsp **basil** (or more)
1 **bay leaf**	**salt and freshly ground pepper**
2-3 cloves **garlic**	6-7 **tomatoes** (or more if canned) cut up
3 **carrots**	into chunky pieces
2 small stalks **celery**	1/2 lb **shell macaroni or rotini**
1 large **onion**	**fresh parsley**, chopped
3 tbsp **olive oil**	**parmesan cheese**, grated

- Combine the beans with 6 cups water in a saucepan. Add salt, olive oil, bay leaf and whole garlic cloves.
- Let simmer 2-3 hours until tender. Add water as necessary to cover.
- Discard the bay leaf, *smush* up the garlic, pour off and reserve the liquid.
- Scrape and dice the carrots, slice the celery and chop the onions.
- Saute in hot olive oil in a large skillet with the garlic and herbs.
- Add the tomatoes, cover and let cook 10-15 minutes.
- Combine the beans with the cooked vegetables and as much of the reserved bean stock as you like without making the sauce too soupy.
- Cook the macaroni.
- Combine the macaroni with the beans and vegetables in a big bowl.
- Toss with parmesan cheese, and sprinkle parsley over the top.
- Serve immediately.

PART TWO
OUR EXPERTS' RECIPES

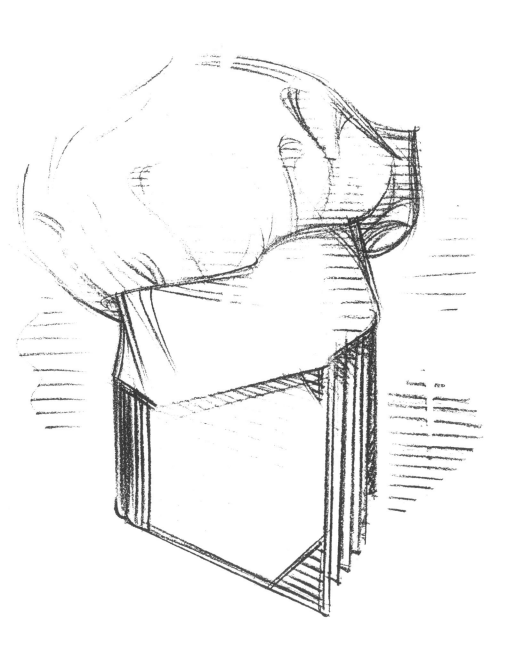

THE BEST OF *B*RIDGE

The Best of Bridge Publishing Ltd is seven remarkable women: Karen Brimacombe, Marilyn Lyle, Mary Halpen, Linda Jacobson, Helen Miles, Valerie Robinson, Joan Wilson.

The five cookbooks published by this Calgary bridge club have been consistent best sellers since the women published the first in the series, **The Best of Bridge**, in 1976. Sales have exceeded 2,000,000 copies and the company grosses over $1,000,000 annually.

The group of bridge players turned authors were friends for twelve years before they became business partners, turning their love of cooking into a profitable venture from the beginning. Filled with "simple recipes with gourmet results" and humorous one liners in a hand lettered format, the cookbooks have become as much of a staple as sugar in North American households.

Since their first book, the seven women have published four more wonderful collections of tried, true and thoroughly tested recipes. **Enjoy!** was released in 1979, **Winners** in 1984 and **Grand Slam** in 1988. Their fifth book, **Aces**, debuted in 1992 when the Best of Bridge women were featured at the Festival of the Written Arts. As with its four predecessors, **Aces** was written, published, promoted and distributed by their own company.

The seven Calgary authors laugh when they reply to the four most frequently asked questions: "Yes, we're still good friends. No, we're not all divorced. Yes, we've made money. And no, we don't play bridge anymore!"

Festival 10 (1992)

STACKED PIZZA

from their cookbook **Aces**. (For adults only.)

7 sheets **phyllo pastry**
1/2 cup **butter,** melted 125 mL
7 tbsp **freshly grated parmesan cheese** 105 mL
1 1/2 cups **grated mozzarella cheese** 375 mL
1 **onion,** thinly sliced
5 - 6 **Roma tomatoes,** sliced
1 tsp **oregano** 5 mL
salt & pepper to taste
fresh herb sprigs of thyme, oregano, rosemary

- Preheat oven to 375°F. To thaw and prepare phyllo, follow package instructions.
- Place first sheet of phyllo on baking sheet, brush with butter and sprinkle with one tbsp parmesan cheese. Repeat until all sheets are used. Press firmly so layers will stick togther.
- Sprinkle top sheet with mozzarella and onions. Arrange tomato slices on top. Season with oregano, salt and pepper.
- Bake for 20 - 25 minutes, until edges are golden. Decorate with herbs and cut into squares.
- Note: olives, anchovies and/or peppers can also be used, but don't overload as this is a delicate crust!

BROCCOLI MANDARIN SALAD

From their cookbook **Aces**.

DRESSING
2 **eggs**
1/2 cup **sugar** 125 mL
1 tsp **cornstarch** 5 mL
1 tsp **dry mustard** 5 mL

1/4 cup **white wine vinega**r 60 mL
1/4 cup **water** 60 mL
1/2 cup **mayonnaise** 125 mL

SALAD
4 cups **fresh broccoli florets** 1 L
1/2 cup **raisins** 125 mL
8 slices **bacon,** cooked & chopped
2 cups **sliced fresh mushrooms** 500 mL

1/2 cup **slivered toasted almonds** 125 mL
10 oz can **mandarin oranges,** drained 284 mL
1/2 **red onion,** sliced

- To make dressing: In a saucepan, whisk together eggs, sugar, cornstarch and dry mustard. Add vinegar and water and cook slowly until thickened. Remove from heat and stir in mayonnaise. Cool.
- To make salad: Marinate broccoli in dressing for several hours. Add remaining ingredients and toss well.
- Serves 6.

GRAND SLAM FINALE

From their cookbook **Grand Slam**.

1 cup **Vanilla wafer cookie crumbs** 250 mL
　　(24 wafers)
1/2 cup **toasted almonds,** finely chopped 125 mL
1/4 cup **butter,** melted 50 mL
4 cups **fresh strawberries** 1 L
12 oz **good quality white chocolate** 375 g
4 oz **cream cheese** 125 g
1/4 cup **sugar** 50 mL
1/4 cup **orange liqueur or frozen orange juice concentrate** 50 mL
1 tsp **vanilla** 5 mL
2 cups **whipping cream** 500 mL
2 tbsp **cocoa powder** 25 mL

- Combine wafer crumbs, almonds and butter. Press into bottom of 9" springform pan.
- Wash, dry and hull berries. Reserve a few for garnish.
- Chop chocolate and melt in double boiler or microwave. Spread 3 tbsp chocolate over cookie base. Arrange whole berries, points up, on base. Refrigerate.
- Allow remaining chocolate to cool slightly. Beat cheese until smooth, then beat in sugar. Mix in liqueur (or juice) and vanilla. Slowly beat in remaining chocolate. Whip cream. Stir about 1/3 into chocolate mixture and fold in the remainder.
- Pour over berries, shaking pan gently to fill in between berries. Refrigerate 3 hours or overnight. To remove, run knife carefully around edge and gently remove from springform. Dust with cocoa and garnish with reserved strawberries.

DIANE  LEMENT

Diane Clement is the author of 4 Canadian best-selling cookbooks: **Chef On The Run**, and **More Chef On The Run**. Her third book, written with husband Dr. Doug Clement, was the health-conscious **Chef And Doctor On The Run** (Sunflower Publications, 1986) which sold 10,000 copies in Canada in its first week of sales. **Fresh Chef on the Run** (Sunflower), another healthy lifestyle inspired cookbook, was published in 1990. Diane's cooking credentials include study at La Varenne in Paris and she has attended Cordon Bleu in London, New York and other cities worldwide for sessions with international chefs. She is a member of the International Association of Cooking Professionals and a founding member of the B.C. Chapter of Les Dames d'Escoffier International.

In 1991 Diane opened *The Tomato Fresh Food Cafe* with her actress daughter Jennifer and partners Jamie Norris and Haik Gharibians.

But there is another side to this lady: she is a former sprinter on the Canadian Olympic Team (1956) and winner of a bronze medal in the 1958 Commonwealth Games. Since she retired as a sprinter she has served as coach and past president of the Canadian Track and Field Association, Team Manager (Athletics) for the Canadian team at the 1984 Los Angeles Olympics, and Team Manager (Athletics) for Canada at the 1988 Seoul Olympics. She still remains very active in sports, jogging and exercising daily.

Diane's husband, Dr. Doug Clement, with whom she wrote **Chef and Doctor on the Run**, represented Canada in the 400 and 800 metre race at the 1952 and 1956 Olympics and won a silver medal in the 1954 Commonwealth Games. Today he is co-director of the Allan McGavin Sports Medicine Centre and Professor in the Faculty of Medicine at the University of B.C. He has an active practice in sports medicine and conducts research in the area of exercise-induced injuries and sports nutrition. Doug received the Order of Canada in 1991.

Festival 8 (1990)

DIANE'S CORNBREAD

This bread goes great with soups, chili, salads, etc. or just on its own for a quick pick-me-up! One of our *Tomato Fresh Food Cafe*'s favourites.

5 cups **white flour**
3 cups **cornmeal**
1/2 cup **white sugar**
1 tsp **salt**
6 1/2 tbsp **baking powder**
  (Yes, that's really tablespoons!)
2 cups **sharp low fat cheddar cheese,**
  grated
2 cups **frozen corn niblets**

5 large **eggs**
1 litre **buttermilk**
1 cup **chopped canned green mild chillies**

• In one large bowl, mix the first seven ingredients in the order listed. Blend well.
• Add the remaining 3 ingredients. Mix all gently to blend.
• Pour into large lasagne-sized pan sprayed with cooking oil spray. Bake at 375˚F for about 40 to 45 minutes or more until firm and golden. Serve warm. Yields 15 servings.

Nutrient Analysis (per serving):
Carbohydrate   73 g
Protein   15 g
Fat   5 g
Energy   397 calories

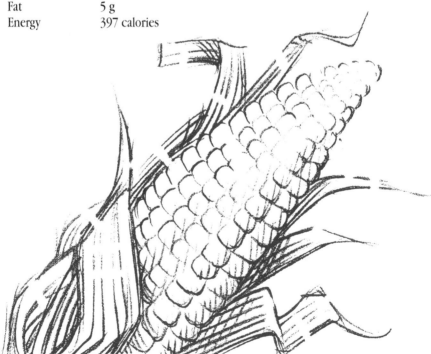

SUSAN MENDELSON

On December 14, 1979, Susan Mendelson and a partner opened their doors to the public as *The Lazy Gourmet,* a gourmet take-out food store and catering business on Vancouver's West Fourth Avenue. For the first seven months they literally "did it all". They worked seven days a week, sixteen hours a day—shopping, cooking, selling, washing dishes, and keeping the books. Theirs was the first store of its kind in western Canada and people came from miles around to buy their incomparable cheesecakes, tortes, and prepared gourmet foods to go. By the end of the first year they were able to hire a dish washer and a small catering staff to do outside catering.

In 1980 Susan came out with her first book: **Mama Never Cooked Like This** which brought even more attention to their now successful store. The partners appeared on *The Vancouver Show* every other Friday doing cooking demonstrations, and Susan did a bi-weekly spot on CBC Radio. In 1982 she wrote her children's cookbook, **Let Me in the Kitchen**; 1983's book was a collaboration entitled **Nuts About Chocolate**. A year later the partners completed a fresh fruit cookbook called **Fresh Tarts**.

Susan's **Expo '86 Cookbook** was a hit of Vancouver's Expo '86 year; in 1992 she co-authored **Still Nuts About Chocolate**. And in 1994 Susan Mendelson and her sister Rena Mendelson will publish **Food To Grow On**.

Meanwhile in 1988 Susan had bought out her Lazy Gourmet partner to become the sole owner. She bought *Bridges Bagel Deli* in April 1992 and turned it into the *Lazy Gourmet Cafe,* serving breakfast, lunch and dinner seven days a week. It will soon feature an extensive take-out area and will continue to expand the already high volume catering business that the *Lazy Gourmet* has become famous for.

Susan continues to write for national cooking magazines, local magazines and newspapers. In addition, she has still found time to serve on the board of governors of the Vancouver Playhouse since 1987, as secretary in 1992-3 and vice president since then, and on the Gala Committee for the Vancouver International Wine Festival since 1990.

Festival 2 (1984)

TRIPLE BERRY CRISP PIE

(from **Food to Grow On** by Susan and Rena Mendelson)

9 inch **deep-dish pie crust,** prebaked
2 cups **sliced peaches**
2 cups **raspberries**
  (berries may be fresh or frozen)

2 cups **blueberries**
1 cup **sugar**
3 tbsp **cornstarch**
1/4 tsp **nutmeg**

• Mix together in large bowl. Pour into baked pie crust.

TOPPING:
3/4 cup **flour**
3/4 cup **brown sugar**

1 cup **quick-cooking oats**
1/2 cup **cold butter**

• Rub together to form crumbs.
• Spread topping over berries.
• Place pie on cookie sheet (to catch runover juice)
• Bake in pre-heated oven 375°F for 7 - 9 minutes.

THAI SPINACH SALAD

(from **Food to Grow On** by Susan and Rena Mendelson)

1 **large head spinach**
1 cup **fresh bean sprouts**
1 **red pepper,** sliced

1/2 cup **white mushrooms,** slivered
1/2 cup **slivered toasted almonds**

• Remove stems and wash the spinach, chop into slivers.
• Add other ingredients.

DRESSING:
6 tbsp **lime juice**
1/4 cup **brown sugar**
1 tsp **chinese chili garlic sauce**
1 tbsp **freshly minced gingerroot**

2 tbsp **mint leaves,** minced
2 tbsp **fresh basil,** minced
1/4 tsp grated **nutmeg**
1/2 cup **peanut oil**

• Mix well. Use only half the dressing and save the rest for another day.

UMBERTO MENGHI

Umberto Menghi has been called the restaurant king of Vancouver, but besides being a restaurant owner, he is the host of a syndicated cooking show, the originator of a chain of fast food pasta franchises, and the author of **The Umberto Menghi Cookbook** (1982), **Umberto's Pasta Book** (1985), and **The Umberto Menghi Seafood Cookbook** (1987).

Born in Florence, Italy, in 1946, Umberto Menghi was destined for the seminary, his parents' choice for their youngest son, but instead at sixteen he enrolled in a hotel school in Rome. Absorbing all the secrets of the world of cuisine as he went along, he headed for London and then France to continue his training.

Arriving in Canada in time for Expo'67, Umberto Menghi went to work in Montreal's Queen Elizabeth Hotel; when Expo was over, he headed west to Vancouver. Two unsuccessful restaurant ventures were followed by the opening in 1973 of

Umbertos, the little yellow house on Hornby Street, and Vancouver was never the same. Opening night was frantic in the tiny 50-seat restaurant when Umberto had to ask his customers to front cash so he could run out and buy wine, but the near disaster turned into a party with very impressive fare. When he told everyone to pay only what they thought the dinner was worth, the evening grossed an impressive $5,200!

Since the opening of his first restaurant, Umberto Menghi has devoted his life to cooking and to his belief in the simple basics of good food. His restaurants now also include *Il Giardino* (opened in 1976), *Al Porto* (1978), *Il Caminetto* in Whistler, B.C. (1981), *Umbertos* in San Francisco (1984), *Settebello* on Vancouver's Robson Street (1986), *Trattoria di Umberto* in Whistler (1987), *Umberto's Grill* in Whistler (1989), and *Splendido* on Robson Street (1991).
Festival 9 (1991)

OSSO BUCO (BRAISED VEAL SHANK)

6 **Veal shin bones well covered in meat**   1/4 cup **flour** 50 g
salt to taste   1/4 cup **olive oil or vegetable oil** 50 ml
black pepper, freshly ground to taste

- Preheat oven to 350°F.
- Season veal with salt and pepper.
- Dip veal in flour, shaking off the excess.
- Saute veal on all sides in hot oil in a large skillet on medium heat until brown to seal in the meat's juices.
- Put veal in a casserole dish just big enough to contain the meat.

SAUCE:

1 tsp **olive oil** 5 ml
1 tsp **butter** 5 g
1 large **onion,** finely chopped
1 medium **carrot,** finely chopped
1 stalk **celery,** finely chopped
2 cloves **garlic,** finely chopped
1 cup **dry red wine** 250 ml

32 oz can peeled Italian tomatoes,
    finely chopped 900ml
      or equivalent fresh tomatoes, and their liquid
salt to taste
black pepper, freshly ground, to taste
1 tsp **brown sugar**   5 g
gremolata (See below)

- Saute onion in oil and butter in another skillet on medium heat until onion is transparent.
- Add carrot, celery and garlic to onion and saute on medium heat for 5 minutes.
- Add wine, tomatoes and their liquid and brown sugar to onion, carrots, celery, and garlic. Stir until well blended.
- Season with salt and pepper.
- Cover veal with sauce and put casserole dish, covered, in oven.
- Bake at 350°F for 1 1/2 hours.
- Bake uncovered for the last 1/2 hour.
- Put veal on a warm serving platter or on warm plates.
- Sprinkle with gremolata and serve.

GREMOLATA:

2 tsp **lemon peel,** grated 10 g
1 clove **garlic,** finely chopped
4 tsp **fresh parsley,** finely chopped 20 g

- Mix lemon peel, garlic and parsley together in a bowl.

This recipe for Osso Buco serves 6 people.

JEAN PARÉ

Jean Paré, author of the **Company's Coming** cookbooks, was born and raised during the Depression years in Irma, a small farm town in eastern Alberta. She grew up understanding that the combination of family, friends and home cooking is the essence of a good life. When she left home she took with her many acquired family recipes, her love of cooking and her desire to read cookbooks like others read novels.

While raising a family of four, Jean's reputation flourished as the mom who would happily feed the whole neighbourhood. In 1963 when her children had all reached school age, she volunteered to cater the dinner for the 50th anniversary of the Vermilion School of Agriculture (now Lakeland College). Working out of her home she prepared a dinner for more than 1000 people and launched a catering operation that would flourish for over eighteen years.

Time and again she was asked, "Why don't you write a cookbook?" Her response was to team up with her son Grant Lovig in the fall of 1980 to form Company's Coming Publishing Limited. On April 14, 1981, **150 Delicious Squares**, the company's first book was published, followed by a cookbook a year for the next five years. The pace speeded up in 1987 with two new titles each year after that.

Her approach to cooking has always called for easy-to-follow recipes using mostly common, affordable ingredients. Her wonderful collection of time-honoured recipes, many of which are family heirlooms, are a welcome addition to any kitchen. That is why the Company's Company motto is: Taste the Tradition.

Jean Paré's cookbook company has grown from the early days when she worked out of a spare bedroom in her home to operating a large and fully equipped test kitchen in Vermilion, near the home she and her husband Larry Paré built. Full time staff has grown steadily to include marketing personnel located in major cities across Canada and the United States. Home Office is located in Edmonton, Alberta, where distribution, accounting and administrative functions are headquartered.

Jean Paré's latest cookbooks are **Light Recipes** and **Microwave Cooking**(1993). There are currently 20 titles in the **Company's Coming** cookbook series.

Festival 7 (1989)

RASPBERRY-MALLOW SQUARES

A gorgeous red ribbon between a white shortbread base and a melted marshmallow top.

CRUST:
1 cup **all-purpose flour**
1/2 cup **butter or margarine**
2 tbsp **granulated sugar**

FILLING:
3 oz **raspberry flavored gelatin**
1 cup **boiling water**
15 oz **frozen raspberries,** partly thawed
32 **large white marshmallows**

1/2 cup **milk**
1 cup **whipping cream**
   (or 1 envelope topping)

- Mix flour, butter and sugar until crumbly.
- Press into ungreased 9 x 9 inch pan.
- Bake in 325°F oven for 15 minutes.
- Stir gelatin and water together until dissolved.
- Add raspberries. Mix together. Chill until syrupy.
- Pour over crumbs. Chill.
- Melt marshmallows in milk in top of double boiler. Cool.
- Whip cream until stiff. Fold into cooled marshmallow mixture.
- Spread over firm raspberry jelly. Chill.
- Cuts into 9 servings.

LAYERED LEMON

So refreshing. Absolutely luscious. A favorite refrigerator dessert.

FIRST LAYER
2 cups **all-purpose flour**
1 cup **butter or margarine**
1 cup **pecans,** finely chopped

SECOND LAYER
2 - 8 oz pkts **cream cheese,** softened
1 cup **icing (confectioner's) sugar**
1 cup **whipping cream** (or 1 envelope topping)

THIRD LAYER
2 **lemon pudding and pie fillings** (each make 1 pie)

FOURTH LAYER
2 cups **whipping cream** (or 2 envelopes topping)
2 tbsp **granulated sugar**
1 tsp **vanilla**

- For the first layer, mix flour, butter and nuts together until crumbly. Press into 9 x 13 inch pan. Bake in 350°F oven for 15 minutes. Cool.
- For the second layer, beat cheese and icing sugar together well. Beat whipping cream until stiff. Fold into cream cheese mixture. Spread over cooled crust.
- For the third layer, prepare lemon pie filling according to directions on package. Cool, stirring often. Pour over cheese layer.
- For the fourth layer, beat cream, sugar and vanilla until stiff. Spread over lemon layer. Garnish with chopped pecans or slivered almonds.
- Makes 15 generous pieces.

SALMON 'CHANTED EVENING

Practically no work to this. Easy to double or triple for several more guests. Makes a special evening.

4 lbs. **large thick salmon fillet with skin**	1/2 tsp **salt**
1/2 cup **salad dressing** (such as Miracle Whip)	1/8 tsp **pepper**
1/4 cup **ketchup**	1/2 tsp **worcestershire sauce**
1/4 cup **brown sugar, packed**	**parsley for garnish**
2 tbsp **lemon juice**	**lemon wedges for garnish**
1 tsp **parsley flakes** (or use fresh)	

- Lay salmon skin side down onto double thickness foil that is long enough to cover top loosely. Put on tray for an easy transfer.
- In small bowl combine all ingredients except parsley and lemon wedges. Stir well. Spread over salmon. May be chilled at this point until needed.
- Lay foil with salmon on medium - hot grill. Now take a skewer and poke holes through salmon right down through foil as well. Do this at 2 inch intervals. Bring foil up over ends of fish but do not do up tight. Leave sides exposed. Close lid.
- Total cooking time is about 20 minutes. Allow 10 minutes per 1 inch thickness plus 5 minutes for foil. To serve cut in 2 inch wide pieces. When you lift pieces skin will remain on the foil. Arrange on warm platter.
- Garnish with parsley and lemon. May also be served direct from barbecue to plate. Serves 8.

NICOLE PARTON

Nicole Parton loves food. She loves preparing it, decorating it, admiring it, eating it and writing about it. In fact, she loves food so much she's considering writing a diet book, for which she's already weighed in with a title and shed enough pounds to share the common-sense secret of how she did it.

Among her culinary weaknesses: Belgian chocolate, Belgian waffles, and Belgian stew. Among her least favourites: Brussels sprouts. Anyone who didn't know would think she was Belgian-born, which is exactly what she was.

Raised in Vancouver, she attended UBC for three years, studying English and writing under such instructors as Eric Nicol, Earl Birney and Margaret Atwood. Nonetheless, it took years before she felt courageous enough to write. Before she tried, she taught school in Manitoba, worked for two Canadian banks, sold perfume and wrinkle removers in department stores, learned to say, "Madam, it smells/looks great on you!" and gave birth to a son and twin daughters in a span of 11 months.

When Nicole finally picked up a pen, she found she couldn't put it down, and began writing extensively for newspapers, magazines, radio and television. That was more than 20 years ago, and she's been writing ever since. The winner of several media awards and a former columnist for the Vancouver *Sun*, she's twice been named one of Vancouver's most influential people by judges who have never seen her with flour on her nose and a fallen souffle in her oven.

Nicole is the author of five best-selling books, the first two of which—**The Answer Book** and **The Answer Book II**, both released by the Vancouver *Sun*—became a Canadian publishing phenomenon, selling 250,000 copies worldwide. Nicole has also written **The Whole Kitchen Kaboodle from A to Z**, **Fast and Easy Company Treats** and **The Galley Gourmet**, the happy result of her experimentation aboard the family boat, *Writer's Cramp*.

Nicole Parton believes in keeping meals tasty but simple; her recipes work equally well on camping trips or in an RV. "The best thing about writing a cookbook," she says, "is that you don't mind eating your words." Her never-before-revealed innermost secret desire? To host a TV cooking show in which celebrity guests do all the work and she does the oooh-ing and ahhh-ing and eating. Just remember. . . You read it here first.

Festival 6 (1988)

SPICED BASMATI RICE

This rice is exquisite - unforgettable flavor and very nutritious.

1 tbsp **oil, preferably Canola**
1/2 cup **onion,** thinly sliced
1 cup **long grain brown basmati rice**
2 cups **chicken stock**
1 tsp **salt** (optional)
2 tbsp **unsalted cashews,**
   toasted & coarsely chopped

2 tbsp **unsalted almonds**
2 tbsp **pine nuts**
1/4 cup **light raisins**
1/4 tsp **nutmeg**
1/4 tsp **cinnamon**
1/8 tsp **cardamom**
freshly ground pepper

- In a large skillet, heat oil and saute onion until soft. Add raw rice and cook 2 - 3 minutes, stirring constantly.
- In a medium pan, heat stock to boiling. Add rice and onion mixture. Bring to a boil, cover and simmer 45 minutes.
- Turn cooked rice into serving casserole. Toss with nuts, raisins and spices. Season. Serve hot.
- Serves 6

CPR SALAD DRESSING

Years ago, this was the CPR's secret recipe for a great and easy salad dressing. I obtained it through a source who shall remain nameless. Once you've tried it, you'll make it over and over again.

1/2 cup **oil, preferably Canola**
1/4 cup **malt vinegar**
1 tsp **paprika**
1 tsp **salt**
1/2 cup **white sugar**

1/3 cup **ketchup**
1 tbsp **dried minced onion**
   or 2 tbsp. **fresh onion,** finely chopped
1 tbsp **lemon juice**

- Zap in a blender and serve. This lasts a couple of months in the fridge, in a covered container.

Eat your heart out, Paul Newman!

PART THREE
THE FESTIVAL'S OWN RECIPES

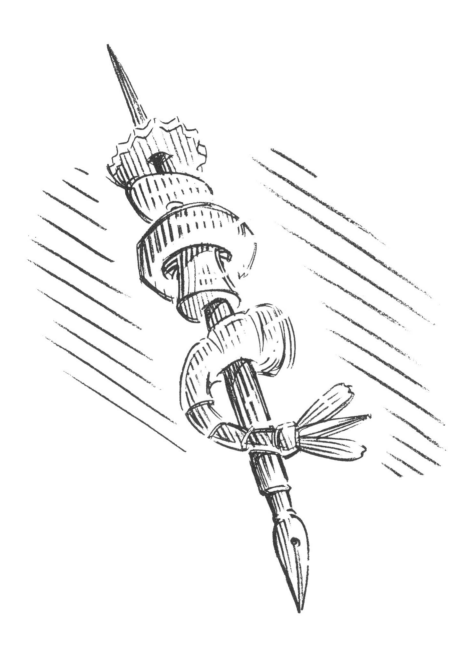

BROCCOLI SOUP

This is staple fare with a gourmet touch for our Writers in Residence participants. No workshop is complete without it.

4 tbsp **margarine**
4 large **onions,** chopped
2 cloves **garlic,** chopped
3 tsps **curry powder,** or more to taste
freshly ground black pepper to taste
4 cups **chicken broth**
4 cups **water**
4 lbs **broccoli,** cut into flowerets, stems cut into 1/2 inch slices
4 large **potatoes,** peeled and cut into 1/2 inch cubes
4 cups **milk, skim or low-fat**

- In a large saucepan, melt the margarine, and saute the onion and garlic for a few minutes.
- Add the curry, pepper, broth and water to the pan, and bring the soup to a boil.
- Add the broccoli and potato. When the mixture returns to a boil, reduce the heat, cover the pan, and simmer the soup for about 20 minutes or until the vegetables are tender.
- Puree the soup in batches in a blender or food processor. Return the puree to the pan, stir in the milk, and cook the soup over low heat until it is hot (but do not boil).
Serves 24

QUILLER'S RED LENTIL SOUP

This recipe was given to our chef Gwen Southin by Quiller Treloar, a friend of over 40 years. He and his wife Peggy are now retired at Half Moon Bay, just outside of Sechelt.

8 cups **red lentils**
3 tsp **salt**
8 cups **water**
2 **bay leaves**
3 tbsp **margarine**
1 tsp **garlic,** chopped
8 cups **chicken stock**

2 med **onions,** sliced
8 stlks **celery,** chopped
2 tbsp **marjoram**
2 tbsp **summer savoury**
salt and pepper to taste
28oz can **tomatoes,** chopped
1 cup **skim or low-fat milk**

- Wash lentils. Place in saucepan, add water, bay leaf, a little salt and cook gently until tender.
- In large saucepan, saute onion in margarine and then add all the other ingredients, cook slowly for 15 minutes.
- Stir in lentils and stock.
- Heat gently.

Note: The original recipe called for cream, but for Writer-In-Residence menus we use only skim or low-fat milk.

VEGETABLE CURRY

This is a great favourite at our W.I.R. programs. We make it for the vegetarian students, but it's hard to keep the meat-eaters out of it, too.

2 medium **carrots,** thinly sliced
2 cups **potatoes,** cubed
2 large **onions,** thinly sliced
1 **green pepper,** thinly sliced
2 cups **cauliflower,** cut into flowerets
1 medium **zucchini,** sliced
1 cup **tomatoes,** chopped
16 oz can **chickpeas**

1/2 cup **vegetable broth**
1/4 cup **tomato sauce**
2 cloves **garlic,** minced
2 tbsp **curry powder**
1 tsp **cumin**
1 tbsp **oil**
salt and pepper to taste

- Heat the oil in a skillet or Dutch oven, add the curry, cumin, garlic, salt and pepper.
- Stir in the broth, and cook the mixture for 2 minutes.
- Add the carrots, potatoes, green pepper, onions, and cauliflower.
- Cover the pan and simmer the curry for 5 - 7 minutes or until the vegetables are tender-crisp.
- Add the zucchini, tomatoes, tomato sauce, and chickpeas. Cover the pan, and simmer the curry for 10 minutes.
- Serves 8

HOT SALSA CHICKEN

This began as a mildly tomato-sauced chicken dish, and just got hotter as the years went by.

8 fryer **chickens,** skinned and cut up into small pieces	4 **peppers,** chopped
1/4 cup **oil**	1/2 lb **mushrooms,** sliced
28 oz can **tomatoes,** chopped	2 cans **green chillies**
28 oz can **tomato sauce**	2 cans **pimentos**
2 cups **chicken broth**	4 cloves **garlic,** minced
2 large **onions,** chopped	1 tbsp **chili powder** or more as desired
	1\2 cup **flour**

- Heat oven to 350°F.
- Arrange chicken pieces in large roasting pans and cook for half an hour, turning pieces over once.
- Saute the onions and garlic in the oil.
- Add chili powder and stir.
- Add all other ingredients, mashing down the tomatoes well.
- Simmer over low heat for 5 - 10 minutes.
- Drain fat from chicken.
- Cover chicken with sauce and cook until chicken is tender and no longer pink inside (at least one hour.)
- Thicken with 1\2 cup of flour mixed with water, if desired.
- Serves 24

FESTIVAL CHILI

We make two batches of this chili, one is con carne (with meat), the other vegetarian.

3 large **onions,** chopped	3 cups **carrots,** sliced
3 cloves **garlic,** minced	3 cups **celery,** diced
3 tbsp **oil**	3 cups **corn kernels** (optional)
2 lbs **lean ground beef** (if you're making it con carne)	6 tbsp **chili powder**
	1 tbsp **cumin**
3 28 oz cans **tomatoes,** coarsely chopped	2 tbsp **oregano leaves,** crumbled
2 28 oz **tomato sauce**	2 tsp **ground cloves**
3 28 oz cans **kidney beans**	1 tsp **allspice**
3 - 114ml cans **green chillies**	**salt and peppe**r to taste
3 cups **green peppers,** diced	

- In a large Dutch oven, saute the onion and garlic in the oil until soft.
- Add meat (if using), browning it and stirring to break up the pieces.
- Drain off excess fat. Add tomatoes, tomato sauce and all the seasonings.
- Heat until bubbly, lower heat and simmer for about 30 minutes.
- Add all other ingredients and cook until carrots are soft.
- Makes 24 extra-hearty servings

SEAFOOD NEWBERG

This dish is a favourite of our Writers in Residence participants. There's enough here to feed 24 healthy, hard-working writers or 30 loggers! Note: Prepare it first thing in the morning and refrigerate it for the day so the flavours will meld.

2 cups **margarine**

5 **small onions** (or three medium onions)

1 3/4 cups **flour**

5 cups **whipping cream,** heated
  (do not allow to boil)

5 cups **cold milk**

5 - 10 fl oz cans **cream of mushroom soup**

5 tsp **dry mustard**

8 tbsp **curry powder**

1 1/4 tsp **powdered ginger**

1 1/4 tsp **turmeric**

2 1/2 tsp **lemon juice**

1 tsp **tabasco sauce**

1 1/4 tsp **thyme**

2 1/2 tsp **salt**

2 tsp **white pepper**

1 cup **each red and green pepper,**
  finely chopped

1 1/2 lbs **fresh shrimp or prawns**

5 lbs **fresh crab meat** (or imitation crab meat)

5 - 7 lbs **fresh fish**
  (red snapper, cod or salmon are all suitable)

Topping:

3 cups **old cheddar cheese,** grated

2 1/2 cups **fine dry bread crumbs**

2 1/2 tsp **garlic powder**

1/2 cup **each red and green pepper,** chopped

- Melt margarine in very large saucepan; add onion and saute lightly. Remove from heat and stir in flour. Gradually stir in hot cream.
- Combine milk and mushroom soup and stir into cream mixture. Cook, stirring constantly, over medium heat until mixture just comes to the boil and is thickened.
- Remove saucepan from heat and add mustard, curry, ginger, turmeric, lemon juice, tabasco sauce, thyme, salt, pepper and chopped peppers.
- Cool and add shrimp, crab and fish. Taste and adjust seasoning if necessary.
- Turn mixture into 12"x 20" baking pan.
- For topping, combine all ingredients. Sprinkle over top of casserole. Refrigerate 6 to 8 hours to absorb flavours.
- Bake at 350°F for 40 - 60 minutes or until bubbly. Serve with rice or couscous.

GWEN'S EASY FLUFFY RICE

We offer this for those who find rice-cooking a mystery! The quantities are up to you.

- Fill a large, very heavy pot with water and bring water to a rolling boil.
- Place rice in a sieve and wash under running water.
- Put rice into pot of boiling water; adding a little margerine to prevent it from boiling over.
- Boil uncovered for 15 - 20 minutes.
- Test for doneness.
- As soon as it's done, immediately drain rice in colander and rinse it with hot water.
- Put rice quickly back into cooking pot and cover with a clean towel. Place the pot lid on top of the towel.
- It can be left as much as a 1/2 hour and remain piping hot and ready to serve.

FESTIVAL BARBECUED SALMON

Our annual Volunteers Barbecue features this succulent fare with an array of salads, and of course, a very special cake decorated by Sylvia Blackwell for dessert.

60 lbs **salmon fillets (skin on)**

Marinade:

9 cups **olive oil**

6 3/4 cups **lemon juice**

3 3/8 cups **fresh dill,** finely chopped
  (or 1 1/8 cups dried dill weed)

1/2 cup **grated lemon rind**

salt and pepper

- Cut salmon into serving size pieces.
- Prepare marinade by whisking together olive oil, lemon juice, dill, lemon rind, salt and pepper.
- Pour marinade into shallow containers, arrange fillets in marinade and turn each piece to coat evenly. Cover with plastic wrap and refrigerate.
- Turn each piece after 15 minutes, then marinate them for another 15 minutes. Be careful not to leave them in the marinade longer than a half hour as the acids in the marinade will partially cook the fish, and it will dry out during barbecuing.
- Place fillets on the grill, skin side up, about 6 inches from the hot coals. Baste with marinade. Cook for approximately ten minutes. Turn fillets and cook until fish flakes easily.

BARBECUED SPARERIBS

Picture yourself on a Saturday evening at the Festival of the Written Arts, dining al fresco on a plate of our special spareribs, prepared right there in the garden. Then it's off to the Pavilion to hear the Bruce Hutchison Lecture.

120 lbs **pork spareribs**

- Prepare the spareribs for barbecuing by cutting them into individual serving size pieces. Pre-cook the ribs by baking in the oven for 1 1/2 hours or boiling gently for an 1 1/2 hours. Cool, spread with Maureen's Heavenly Sweet and Sour Sauce and place on the grill over glowing coals. Cook until they are a rich brown on the first side, then turn and cook the second side.
- Serve with baked potatoes, rice or couscous, and a big green salad. Dessert? Festival carrot cake!

Maureen's Heavenly Sweet and Sour Sauce:

30 cups **ketchup**	10 tsp **ground ginger**
13 1/2 cups **packed brown sugar**	(or better yet, sliced ginger root)
13 1/2 cups **white sugar**	20 **lemons**
10 tsp **cinnamon**	

- Mix first five ingredients in saucepan. Squeeze lemons and add juice to saucepan. Mix well bringing sauce to a boil over low heat and cook for 45 minutes, stirring occasionally. Set aside to cool.
- Refrigerated, this sauce keeps for six months!

This spareribs recipe serves 240 reasonably hungry people or 160 ravenous ones!

FESTIVAL CARROT CAKE

In the last five years, we have probably made over 200 of these cakes, each one of them big enough to provide 20 to 25 people with a satisfying dessert. Note that the carrots are cooked and pureed BEFORE they go into the batter, an innovation we learned from **The Silver Palate Cookbook**.

3 3/4 cups **all purpose flour**
3 3/4 cups **granulated sugar**
1 1/4 tsp **salt**
1 1/4 tbsp **baking soda**
1 1/4 tbsp **ground cinnamon**
1 7/8 cups **corn oil**

5 **large eggs,** lightly beaten
1 1/4 tbsp **vanilla**
1 7/8 cups **shredded coconut**
1 2/3 cups **pureed cooked carrots**
1 cup **crushed pineapple,** drained

- Preheat oven to 350°F. Grease a 12" x 18" cake pan.
- Sift dry ingredients into a bowl.
- Add oil, eggs and vanilla. Beat well.
- Fold in coconut, carrots and pineapple.
- Pour batter into the prepared pan. Set on the middle rack of the oven and bake for approximately 45 minutes, until edges have pulled away from the sides of the pan and a cake tester inserted in centre comes out clean.
- Makes 20 to 25 serving. May be served with ice cream or whipped cream, or iced with lemon or cream cheese icing.

WRITERS' SPECIAL COFFEE CAKE

We serve this for morning and afternoon coffee breaks to keep up our writers' strength.

1 cup **sugar**
6 tbsp **shortening**
3 **eggs, beaten**
1 tsp **salt**

6 tsps **baking powder**
4 cups **flour**
2 cups **milk**
2 tsp **vanilla**

Topping:
3 tsp **cinnamon**
2 cups **chopped nuts, walnuts or slivered almonds**
3/4 cup **brown sugar**
3/4 cup **white sugar**

- Combine all ingredients for topping.
- Grease and flour a 12" x 20" pan.
- Blend sugar and shortening together. Stir in beaten egg.
- Mix salt, baking powder and flour together.
- Add vanilla to milk and add to batter alternately with dry ingredients.
- Spread a little of batter into prepared pan.
- Sprinkle half of topping on top of batter.
- Cover with remaining batter and sprinkle with remaining topping.
- Bake in a moderate over 350°F for about 1 hour.
- Allow to sit for 15 minutes before serving.
- Serves 24.

About the Festival of the Written Arts

On August 3, 1983, with not much more to recommend them than high hopes and a shoestring budget, the members of the SunCoast Writers' Forge—the Sunshine Coast's writers network—launched the first Festival of the Written Arts in Sechelt's Arts Centre. When it was all over, the books showed a shortfall of $1,600, but it is to the Forge members' great credit, that in spite of the deficit (and not much more heartening financial showings on the next three festivals), they persevered.

Believing that many Canadian writers of superior talent are underpromoted and therefore often little known in their own country, the Festival's founders resolved right from the beginning to present only Canadian writers, editors and publishers. The six events of that first year showcased such British Columbia writers as novelist Jack Hodgins, poet Dorothy Livesay, playwright Leonard Angel and children's writer Florence McNeil, and it established the format that would be followed so successfully in subsequent years: individual hour-and-forty-five minute showcases for each writer with a Saturday noon-time panel discussion to thrash out Canada's literary and cultural problems. The founders also made sure their audiences had plenty of access to the writers they had come to hear by scheduling suppers and lunches and evening receptions to bring everyone together.

The success of the first festival forced a relocation the following year to Greene Court Recreation Centre which had a much larger hall. By the third festival, the budget allowed them to invite authors from beyond our provincial borders. And when the popularity of the festival continued to grow, the organizers rented the gym of the nearby elementary school to house the audiences who came to hear writers like W.O. Mitchell, Peter Gzowski and John Gray. By 1987 even the gym wasn't large enough, and a 400-seat tent was erected beside the hall at Greene Court. During these years the festival played host to P.K. Page, George Ryga, L.R.Wright, Al Purdy, Edith Iglauer, Allan Fotheringham, Christie Harris, David Suzuki, Lynn Bowen, Knowlton Nash, Sara Ellis, W.P.Kinsella and many, many more of Canada's great writers.

On April 15, 1987, just before the fifth festival, the Festival of the Written Arts separated from the Suncoast Writers' Forge and incorporated as a new society, although Festival leadership remained with the Forge members who had organized the festivals from their inception. At this time, in addition to the annual festival, the new society undertook a second project: a series of writers-in-residence workshops.

By 1988 and the sixth Festival of the Written Arts, it had become a 3 1/2 day 15-event celebration that included readings by poets, newspaper columnists, novelists, romance writers, sports writers, playwrights, short story writers, biographers, historians, environmentalists and children's writers, organized with careful attention to a balance of well-known names and future writing stars. But that 6th festival made it plain that the time had come to move to a new venue; the size of our audiences had outstripped the size of available tents. The Festival of the Written Arts needed a permanent home, and the board of directors looked toward the Rockwood Centre as the obvious solution.

Located on the rise of ground to the west of Sechelt village, the Rockwood Centre's main building is a 60-year-old lodge built to accommodate holidayers arriving via the old Union Steamship line. Set in two acres of rhododendrons, magnolias and evergreens, it provides quiet seclusion although it is only five minutes walk from the shops and the sea. The buildings and property had been acquired by the District Municipality of Sechelt in 1987, so with the municipal council's blessing, the Festival Society constructed an outdoor pavilion in a grove of cedars and firs in the northeast corner of the grounds. The last paving bricks were set into the entranceway just thirty minutes before the ribbon cutting ceremony took place at Festival #7.

Constructed entirely of B.C. fir and cedar, the completed pavilion is set into the hillside to take advantage of the natural slope for its 465 seats. It is, according to columnist Charles Lynch (Festival '89), "one of the wonders of the Coast." The Festival Society now schedules a series of at least nine concerts during the summer months, concentrating principally on jazz and light classics.

In the fall of 1991 corporate and private sponsors made it possible for the Festival Society to install a permanent stepped concrete floor with lighting units set into the aisles. In addition the Sunshine Coast Musical Society constructed a pit in front of the stage to accommodate an orchestra. It was first used in July 1992 for their production of Anne of Green Gables. As the pit has been designed so that it can be covered when not in use, there is no loss in the number of seats available for festival events.

In 1994 the Festival adds an extra day to "Festival Weekend", presenting four and half days of great Canadian writing events to the public. There will be more workshops for writers, and more light classic and jazz concerts. In 1992 the Festival forged an alliance with the Arts Council's annual Crafts Fair; it is now held during Festival weekend and advertised in the Festival's brochures. In the coming years we hope to find ways in which to showcase more of the Coast's artists at Festival time.

We invite you to share the Festival and all the Centre has to offer with us.